Dive into a poem

Edited by John Howes and Fran Neatherway

Copyright © 2024 The Rugby Cafe Writers.
Copyright remains with the individual writers of each story.
All rights reserved.

This book or any portion thereof may not be reproduced or used in any manner whatsoever without the express written permission of the publisher except for the use of brief quotations in a book review.
Printed in the United Kingdom.

This is a work of fiction. Unless otherwise indicated, all the names, characters, businesses, places, events and incidents in this book are either the product of the author's imagination or used in a fictitious manner. Any resemblance to actual persons, living or dead, or actual events is purely coincidental.

First Printing, 2024

ISBN: 9798336166019
Imprint: Independently published

For more information about The Cafe Writers of Rugby, visit their website, www.rugbycafewriters.com

The text of this book is set in Newsreader, 10.5pt.

Introduction

If you are new to poetry, then this might be a good place to start. This selection is brought to you by more than thirty poets who belong to the Rugby Cafe Writers. We are a group of new and experienced writers who meet every fortnight in the cafe at St Andrew's Church, Rugby in Warwickshire, a mainly rural county in the centre of England.

Some of us have never written poetry before whilst, for others, it is a way of life. Rarely does a day go by when some of us fail to put pen to paper. You may like to try this approach yourself - commit to writing a poem every day based on how you are feeling, something you have experienced or seen, or maybe even something you have dreamt.

We all have a poetic voice within us and the aim of our group is to help people discover that voice. If you are writing a poem, there are no rules. You can make it rhyme if you want to, but you don't have to. You can work to a specific structure of so many syllables per line, or so many lines per verse, but you don't have to. You can use conventional punctuation and spelling if you like, but you don't have to.

Some of the most enjoyable poems in this collection break all the rules – and why shouldn't they? Others stick to a strict rhyming pattern and you can admire the skill of the poet.

So we invite you to dive into our poetry collection and find something you enjoy - and if you feel like diving into writing yourself, then visit our website and find out about how to join our group.

www.rugbycafewriters.com

John Howes

Dive into a poem

Contents

Poetry is... **Wendy Goulstone**	9
We are the Writers... **Theresa Le Flem**	10
The Useless Poet **Martin Curley**	11
Lost in Words **Dean Speed**	12
If **Ruth Hughes**	13
The Bells of Dunwich **Christopher Trezise**	16
Gibraltar Point Chris Rowe	18
A Glimpse of Heaven **Wendy Goulstone**	19
I Love to be Beside the Sea **Rosemary Marks**	20
Sandcastles **Theresa Le Flem**	21
Mist **John Howes**	22
At the Boathouse with Dylan Thomas **Wendy Goulstone**	23
Sea Me **EE Blythe**	24
Going Home **Rosemary Marks**	25
Walking with Offa **Wendy Goulstone**	26
A date in a Bedouin tent **Kate A Harris**	27
Doughnuts **Chloe Huntington**	30
21st Century Gin Binge **Caroline Lucy**	31
Shopping **Susan McCranor**	32
Saint Patrick **Fran Neatherway**	33
Lady of Letters **Martin Curley**	34
Just a thought **Ruth Hughes**	35
The Echo Man **Christopher Trezise**	36
Black on White **David G Bailey**	37
The Book Club **Susan McCranor**	38
I Wuz Robbed! **Philip Gregge**	39
A boy named Bill (love) **David G Bailey**	40
A boy named Bill (hate) **David G Bailey**	42
Well, Tuck your Frock **Chris Rowe**	44
Balletic Experience **Ann Cooper**	46
Don't put me in a box **Rosemary Marks**	48
Iron Horse **Patrick Garrett**	49
Railroad Blues **Martin Curley**	50
My final sonnet **Wendy Goulstone**	51
Graham **John Howes**	53
She Knows Her Place **Martin Curley**	54
Stillborn **Brian Haynes**	55
Play with Me **A.A.Malik**	56
Love **Patrick Garrett**	60
As Ash Wednesday Falls on Valentine's Day **Theresa Le Flem**	61
Faith **Raymond Brown**	62

Dive into a poem

Music Lover **Wendy Goulstone**	64
Musical Memories **Rosemary Marks**	65
Desert Island Disc **Raymond Brown**	66
Silver Swan **Rosemary Marks**	67
Left to say **John Howes**	69
The Last Sonnet **Steve Redshaw**	70
Joyce Elizabeth **David G Bailey**	71
A sonnet for Queen Bess **Madalyn Morgan**	72
Heaven-sent **Simon Parker**	73
Howling at the Moon **David G Bailey**	74
How about She Loves You, by the Bard? **Chris Stanley**	75
The Food of Love **Fran Neatherway**	76
Yet Again You Dodged **EE Blythe**	77
It's not that late **Rosemary Marks**	78
Voices from the darkness **Patrick Garrett**	79
Where Did It Go Wrong? **Neleh Yartel**	80
Hope **Raymond Brown**	82
I Miss You So **Caroline Lucy**	83
One Kiss **EE Blythe**	84
To All the Lovers I Never Had **Wendy Goulstone**	85
The Poppy **Patrick Garrett**	86
Blown Up **Geoff Hill**	87
Tess and the Mayor **Martin Curley**	88
Eighty Years On **David G Bailey**	90
The Deafening Sound of Silence **Caroline Lucy**	91
Born and quickly forgotten **Dean Speed**	92
My Perfect Wardrobe **Neleh Yartel**	93
The Cramp **Philip Gregge**	94
Onomato-alphabet **John Howes**	95
Making Plans **Martin Curley**	96
Dry My Tears **Jeremy Sadler-Scott**	98
I don't like Mondays **John Howes**	100
Why Do I Bother? **Rosemary Marks**	101
Gluttony **Ann Cooper**	102
The Winner **Caroline Lucy**	103
The Satnav **Wendy Goulstone**	104
A Sonnet **Kate A Harris**	105
A Non-Sonnet **Chris Rowe**	106
Where did the loving go? **Wendy Goulstone**	108
First time **John Howes**	109
No New Beginnings **EE Blythe**	110
A Lonely Soul **Rosemary Marks**	111
Conversation with a Shaving Mirror **David G Bailey**	114
Designer Shoes **Martin Curley**	115

Dive into a poem

Pandemic 2020 **Patrick Garrett**	117
Lockdown Dreamer **Raymond Brown**	118
Dad's Old Shed **Rosemary Marks**	119
Anthony Edwards **David G Bailey**	120
The Day That Never Was **EE Blythe**	121
Autumn Has Arrived **Neleh Yartel**	122
Dad Two **Red Wellies**	124
Colourful Vibes **Ann Cooper**	125
Waiting for Juliet **Madalyn Morgan**	126
Autumn Girl **EE Blythe**	127
Sharing the Load - Derwentwater **Wendy Goulstone**	128
Bus journey **Kate A. Harris**	129
Oxford Thoughts **Raymond Brown**	131
Transported or The Art of Sitting Still **Wendy Goulstone**	132
Bored and Lodging in UHCW **Jenny Hicks**	133
Old Age **Raymond Brown**	136
Now and Then **Susan McCranor**	137
The daydream **Ann Cooper**	139
Gremlins on the lines **Wendy Goulstone**	140
The Pudding Club **Susan McCranor**	141
So Faithfully Superstitious **Philip Gregge**	142
Trains **John Howes**	143
Last Orders **Wendy Goulstone**	144
Shirley A Thorpe **David G Bailey**	145
Rain **Fran Neatherway**	146
Hail Caesar! The Battle Cry **Madalyn Morgan**	147
Worshiper **Alicja Kulczak**	148
Easter Light **Raymond Brown**	149
We Always Look Up **Jeremy Sadler-Scott**	150
Maggie **Caroline Lucy**	151
Wasted **Martin Curley**	152
The Clown **Raymond Brown**	153
Silver! **Neleh Yartel**	154
Writing **Ruth Hughes**	155
Barnardo's poem **Kate A. Harris**	156
The Sage Said... **EE Blythe**	158
Greek cats **Wendy Goulstone**	160
You Belong To Me **Martin Curley**	161
King Jack **Rosemary Marks**	163
The Park Bench **Patrick Garrett**	164
Bird **Theresa Le Flem**	165
Easebourne **John Howes**	166
Ghost Dog **Martin Curley**	167
Another Storm **Kate A. Harris**	169

Dive into a poem

A Trio of Triolets **Chris Rowe**	170
The Magpie **Susan McCranor**	171
Whiteleaf Barrow – Ridgeway Path **Wendy Goulstone**	172
Norfolk Stars **Raymond Brown**	173
The Black Crow **Martin Curley**	174
Insanity Is **Madalyn Morgan**	175
A Death in the Family **Rosemary Marks**	176
Order Of Service **EE Blythe**	177
Questions and answers **John Howes**	178
Because Of You **Madalyn Morgan**	179
Sleep Well David **David G. Bailey**	180
Rainbows **Patrick Garrett**	183
The Big Garden Birdwatch **Susan McCranor**	186
A Flowery Poem **Kate A Harris**	187
Boy on a Swing **Raymond Brown**	188
Beach Holiday? **EE Blythe**	189
Rainfall **Chris Rowe**	190
Hugging the Trees **Wendy Goulstone**	191
Nothing is impossible **Patrick Garrett**	192
The 2024 Marathon **Kate A. Harris**	193
Phoenix **Raymond Brown**	195
Autumn **Patrick Garrett**	196
Leaves **Ruth Hughes**	197
The beautiful Beech **Ann Cooper**	198
The Tide **Chris Rowe**	199
Twinkle, Twinkle Little Star **Rosemary Marks**	202
Surprising Gain **Raymond Brown**	203
Cold Moon **Patrick Garrett**	204
Winter Views **Ann Cooper**	205
A winter drink **Fiona Fisher**	206
Yuletide Dusk **Chris Rowe**	207
Christmas Past, Present and Future **Kate A Harris**	209
Christmas Story **Patrick Garrett**	211
Christmas Snow **Chris Rowe**	212
Good Old Santa **Keith Marshall**	213
And so we got together **Geoff Hill**	214
Christmas Story **Rosemary** Marks	216
New Year Resolutions **Chris Rowe**	217
Meet the poets	221

Poetry is...

Poetry is a dream, a stream, a gleam of light
that breaks the nightmare of a dark night.
Poetry is an owl's call, a stone wall, a ball of fire
that burns and smoulders in unbearable desire.
Poetry is release, love's cease, peace and war
that tears the head and heart with tooth and claw.
Poetry is madness, gladness, sadness for love's loss,
that heavy-hearted bearing of life's cross.
Poetry is anger, languor, a hanger for sorrow,
that despair that cries, 'There is no tomorrow.'
Poetry is beauty, duty, a fruity mix of flavour
that tempts and changes our dull behaviour.
Poetry is hate, fate, a gate through which
that hidden garden seat provides a quiet niche.
Poetry is hope, a microscope, a rope thrown
that saves from drowning those who are alone.
Poetry is honour, optimism, faith for rich and poor.
With a book of poetry in hand who needs more?

Wendy Goulstone

Dive into a poem

We are the Writers...

We are the quiet people, the writers,
who entertain, we type away in our corners
producing reams and reams of paper
promptly shredded, plots discarded,
line after line of sincere misgivings
amid bursts of creativity, verse
after verse of poetry that may never
ever be heard. We are
the compilers of anecdotes.
We are the script writers who tread softly
the boards of our theatrical minds.
Sleep deprived dreamers, we are
haunted by ghosts of our own making.
We are the romantics, the lovers,
the jealous rivals, the inventors
of passionate envious jealous people.
We are the plotters, the forensic scientists,
the analysts, the criminals, the detectives,
we create problems, cause fights, stir up rivalry,
make enemies, decide on their fate
and strike with our pens.
We are the murderers.

Theresa Le Flem

The Useless Poet

I'm not very good at poetry
The thing is like this you see
The harder I try
I just can't seem to get by
And can never get the last line of the verse to rhyme

It's been like this for years
It often has me in tears
Even when I'm writing a birthday card
And I'm trying really hard
I can't get the last line of the verse to rhyme

Just to make things very clear
I made a resolution in the new year
I thought of rhymes every minute, every hour
And though I summoned up all my willpower
I just couldn't get the last line of the verse to rhyme

So now I'm at my wit's end
I've been slowly driven round the bend
I'm sorry it has come to this
I bid you goodbye with a farewell kiss
I feel so much turmoil, loss and sorrow
I'll probably kill myself tomorrow

Martin Curley

Dive into a poem

Lost in Words

Endless drawl of words pouring from my mind,
Verbal diarrhoea spanning sentence, paragraph, lord, give me a sign!

Word after word firing rapidly, as if from a machine gun,
destroying the sandbag of my story, adjective after adjective, brevity gone!

Taking away the meaning, think I might have lost the plot
of my story and my mind, maybe I should stop.

Meandering river of description eroding my story flow,
Maybe it's time for a break; hopefully, that will pull me away from this writing plateau...

Dean Speed

If

If I should write a poem
It would rhyme
About what was most important
At the time
If by stanza three
It makes no sense to me
I'll tear it up
Until another time.

Ruth Hughes

Dive into a poem

Dive into a poem

Dive into a poem

The Bells of Dunwich

In ages dark on Suffolk's coast
A city large was a host
To eight grand churches built with pride
Where the Bishops of Dunwich did reside
The tolling of the bells could be heard clearly.

Saxons and Angles lived hand in hand
In the capitol of this eastern land
A shining jewel glistening brilliantly
Against the backdrop of a stormy sea
The tolling of the bells could be heard clearly.

The city grew along the shore
And soon would face the drums of war
Against the Danes they could not win
They opened the gates and let them in
The tolling of the bells could be heard clearly.

The Danes brought with them Pagan ways
A god that dwelt beneath the waves
Although time records the Bishop's fall
The eight grand churches still stood tall
The tolling of the bells could be heard clearly.

As the years moved on and on
The people mingled becoming one
With the faith of Christ once more returned
The sea gods effigies all were burned
The tolling of the bells could be heard clearly.

The city prospered once more in glory
And so begins the end of its story
A storm surge hit in twelve eighty-six
Destroying buildings of wood and of bricks
The tolling of the bells could be heard clearly.

Twice more storms hit in the following year
The sea gods' wrath some peasants did fear
The second of these on St. Lucia's day
Flooded the land and washed it away
The tolling of the bells could be heard clearly.

Dive into a poem

One and forty years to rebuild
Mourning the loss the storms had killed
But yet again a storm surge struck
The Dunwich folks had run out of luck
The tolling of the bells could be heard clearly.

The trade that gave this city fame
Over the years began to wane
No longer a city and barely a town
Another storm came and four hundred did drown
The tolling of the bells could be heard clearly.

Fifteen years came and passed
They did not know it would be their last
On St Marcellus' feast day it came to be
A final storm claimed Dunwich to the sea
The tolling of the bells could be heard clearly.

Now this place bleak and desolate
Its forgotten city and its watery fate
The local fishers are often heard to say
Whilst fishing out on Dunwich bay
The tolling of the bells could be heard clearly.

Christopher Trezise

Dive into a poem

Gibraltar Point

Gibraltar point – all space and light
A flatness all around of pale beige sand
And shining distant pale grey sea.
Both stretch out around to fade away
Into far off horizons that are indistinct
And far off, too, some silhouettes,
Dark diamonds on stilts and something lower, rushing round about:
Three tiny humans and – is it a dog?– give reassurance
That I am not quite alone.
Behind me, some way back, the little dune of grey-green
    sea-buckthorn,
Nature's savage version of barbed wire,
And the winding sandy trail that delivered me by thorns unscathed
Into this upturned bowl of shining space,
A figure in a snow globe minus snow,
At peace, before it's seized and shaken.
But I am shaken as I stand alone,
Stirred by this spacious glimmering greyness,
Central in this immensity of misty air
And featureless flat land.
Religions could be invented here.
I stand the centre of this universe
And see those far-off figures fade,
Appear and fade away again in mist.
The mist.
I've heard about these Norfolk mists
Deceiving every sense of where one stands.
I start and turn towards that blurring rise of sharp buckthorn
That barrier between the busy-ness of things
And this inspiring nothingness, where everything is indistinct.
The bushes' orange berries beckon,
Little globes to decorate my hastening return.
Once through that sandy slog, beyond that ridge,
The distant café, coffee, cake
And noisy warm normality
Where friends await in fug.

Chris Rowe

Dive into a poem

A Glimpse of Heaven

Near the mouth of the stream
a long granite outcrop
blocks the view of the sea.

Streaked with bands
of powder-pink feldspar
and garnet-rich gneiss
it protects the meadow
from the winter strike
of Atlantic winds.

This is the Gulf Stream coast.
Grasses ripple, enflamed
by summer sun.

Purple vetch, poppy,
red campion, sorrel,
yellow archangel, buttercup,
scabious, cornflower, harebell
people the ancient earth
with rainbows.

You can find this paradise
on a map of The Hebrides.
Or you can search
your mind, find it there.

Wendy Goulstone

Dive into a poem

I Love to be Beside the Sea

I love to be beside the sea
to see the sea in its glory
The gentle ripples on the sand
the waves washing over my hands
Storms are best seen from afar
as they batter land, engulf stray cars
It's all part of nature's great delight
Her gentleness, power and might

I love to be upon the sea
an ocean liner is the place for me
Or maybe on a smaller boat
across the channel we can float
So it's much easier than flying
No queueing, pushing, barging, vying
for space as we gently bob
and look out for land. It's just the job

I love to look beneath the sea
on those nature programmes on TV
Watch the little fishes swim
the sharks and rays and things that sting
I find it all quite fascinating
but please don't think I am debating
being brave, venturing in
Because you see, I cannot swim

Rosemary Marks

Sandcastles

Sandcastles tumble,
the flag on the top
of the castle slips down
as the walls crumble
to the shrieks of childrens' voices,
but not laughter, not this time
a sunny beach
but a bleak and dangerous place,
not a time to play hide-and-seek,
the rumbling sound of explosions
imitates the gentle approach
of the waves,
But the sound of scatter bombs
stops the childrens' chatter,
imitates the screams of seagulls
but no, they're not gulls,
Families desperately run for shelter
from the sudden storm, the sudden shower
but there's no protection
Buckets and spades collect
the debris of peoples' lives,
No-one's safe in this land
invaded by the tide of territorial hate
that overwhelms the beach
This land, this dry dusty
stretch of sand
is laid to waste by bombs and missiles,
It's not the seaside,
nor is the sea an innocent blue,
He who runs to protect his child
may surely die,
but run he must
as the waves
crash over the castle walls,
but the war washes up and over them all
and carries them away

Theresa Le Flem

Mist

Oh, it was so misty
that Friday night by the sea—
West Bay enveloped in a fog,
the waves unusually silent and listening.
We strolled amid the calm,
waiting expectantly for the roughness to return.
But the white gave way to the blue,
the sky filled with sun,
unadulterated and honest,
fresh as a new-born day.
And it shone into our troubled hearts.
The gulls took flight,
the boats set sail
and we were away,
again.

John Howes

Dive into a poem

At the Boathouse with Dylan Thomas

If only I could write like you I'd say
the steel-cold, keel-cleft, slate-glass sea
bears the weight of frowning goose-grey day.
The tide is out, dull mud sucks below the cliff,
swallows flat-pack slabs of stone.
If I had your ears I would hear ghost-voices
across the open-armed, silver-sandaled estuary.
With your eyes I'd see soap-crazed washing,
parsons, milkmen, barmaids, babies, boats.
Today a shirt limps on the clothesline in your garden;
young men and sleek girls serve tea and scones.
Near the know-all church a couple of tourists,
expecting grandeur, search for your grave,
and I think of my father going gently.

Wendy Goulstone

Dive into a poem

Sea Me

You think you know me
But you have no idea
You can't even see me
As I truly am

As I move, I dance
As if you are not here
To you I give the chance
To look; to see me

                It's not what you think
                It's not what you fear
                I'm not a missing link
                I'm not really here

Green hued skin and eyes
Viridian hair
Sinuous limbs rise
Writhe through the water

A flick of a tail ?
And the vision is lost
Just maybe a lone scale
Turning, falling, gone

                Did you really see
                What it might have been
                Can you see it's Me
                Though I am rarely seen.

EE Blythe

Going Home

When all my days have reached their natural end
When all the gifts life gave me have been spent
I'll return then to my ancestral home

A place of mountains, green and sandy bays
Where the sea creeps and crashes on the shore
When all the gifts life gave me have been spent

I'll say a last farewell to all I've known
And lay me down along the water's edge
Where the sea creeps and crashes on the shore

Grains of sand will chase across my body
Tiny crabs will nip my fingers and toes
As I lay down along the water's edge

The waves will pick me up and toss me gently
Catch me quickly, carry me out to sea
Tiny crabs will nip my fingers and toes

No longer feeling, seeing, hearing, being
When all my days have reached their natural end
The waves will carry me quickly out to sea
And I'll return to my ancestral home

Rosemary Marks

Dive into a poem

Walking with Offa

The dyke stretches north on the edge of memory
from Severn estuary to Prestatyn
where it washes away the dust of miles in the sea,
one hundred and eighty four of them
without a soul to pass the time of day,

Offa beckoned us. Come on, come on,
dig out those boots. Come and see what they saw,
those men who dug the ditch
piled up the earth and rocks
to stop the drift from west to east.

In places now it's disappeared beneath the plough
beneath the tread of boot and hoof
broken up by frost and rain and snow,
but still there is enough
to get the gist of what it took to clamber up.

The footpath since has been new-marked
its fingerprint of history lost
with all the mysteries of tales told and lyrics sung
to ease away the hours of dig and thrust.
All gone, except the ghosts.

Wendy Goulstone

Dive into a poem

A date in a Bedouin tent

Memories of my Egyptian holiday

It's squidgy, this delish date,
Dates grown on gigantic date palm trees
Blazing sun beats down, scorching.
Smells of the East, Bedouin tents.

Memories, eating in the Egyptian tent
Tasting dates, sweet, chewy,
Pervades throughout the mouth.
Earthy tastes, splits into the teeth
Sticky, tacky fingers prized apart.

Relish the taste, renew the memories:
Dubai, sand, uncomfortable camel rides,
Sand, sand everywhere in the desert.
Dates are wrinkled, glossy, stoned.
Licking sticky, datey fingers.

Moisture oozes from the dates
Stuck in the teeth, memories renewed,
Sitting cross-legged on the floor,
A colourful Bedouin rug, Turkish
Colours, low-level tables, goodies.

Tastes amazing sinking to the back
Of the mouth, sticking teeth together,
Dark, dark brown and mixes of lighter brown
Toffee-coloured within, stringy.
Exotic taste, exotic location, Dubai memories.

Smell the smells of hash pipes
Smoke, long colourful pipes, smoking,
Smokey in the tent, eating dates.
Asthmatic, inhaled. Hungry.
Experience, dates, scorching sun, Dubai, desert.

Dive into a poem

Smell of date, how to describe?
Strange earthy smell, play with
Date, sticks to fingers, finish the fruit?
Is it a fruit? Yes, a fruit,
Plate of dates, yum, eaten them, every one!

Kate A Harris

Dive into a poem

Dive into a poem

Doughnuts

I love doughnuts,
I don't have them very often
because they're my guilty pleasure,
but I just love them.
A ring doughnut – pink – with rainbow sprinkles.
They're what I love.
I get protective over my doughnuts
and I do not allow anyone else to eat one
without me eating one too.
I have lost friends over this.
Lost friends over a single ring doughnut with rainbow sprinkles –
goodness people are silly.
I've even thrown doughnut parties,
but only with myself, of course.
When people come to my house,
I hide my loves in a cupboard or a drawer.
I love my doughnut, I don't want to share.

I love doughnuts to the point where
I even have doughnut pyjamas with a matching cushion.
I sit on my sofa in them,
eating my four-pack of pink-iced ring doughnuts from my local shop.
I don't travel very far for them,
only five minutes up the road.
I am sure that Belinda from number 53
likes seeing my doughnut pyjamas.
I hate it when people bring me their doughnuts.
They're not mine and they taste strange.
I want my glazed rings
(the ones you get out of an expensive doughnut box).
I need to treat myself.

Chloe Huntington

Dive into a poem

21st Century Gin Binge

Slamming down the cash for that famous last word.
Pile on the ice, slip in the lime.
Sipping and swirling, squealing, and smirking,
Flirting with the everlasting bitterness while
Swimming lengths round the pink goldfish bowl.

Bewildered, skinny-dipping on the rocks.
Pile on the ice, slip in the lime.
Blow torch away that misery, ignite some madness.
Blue grey juniper bush, prickly and sprawling,
But it beats having sex on the beach.

Caroline Lucy

Shopping

Olive Oil
Cherry Toms
Silver foil
Poppadoms

Eggs, Bacon
Poppy seeds
Anything else
that we may need?

Oh yes, a paper,
milk and bread
I'm in such a rush
I'll lose my head

Just one more thing before I go,
I need a plaster for my toe.
Nearly home, I've been an hour
Oh no, I forgot the flour!

I swear and curse and clench my fist,
I should have made a shopping list.

Susan McCranor

Saint Patrick

St Patrick was a bonny lad.
He sent the snakes far, far away.
The people were happy and glad.
St Patrick was a bonny lad.
He knew the snakes were very bad.
They were all gone within a day.
St Patrick was a bonny lad.
He sent the snakes far, far away.

Fran Neatherway

Lady of Letters

I really fancy you Miss A said Edward G
I'm not Miss A I'm Miss B can't you see
ABC said Edward G It's all the same to me
I really fancy you said Edward G
I think you'd prefer Miss C D or E
No, let us exchange pleasantries under the pleasant trees
I really fancy you Miss A said Edward G
I'm not Miss A I'm miss B can't you see

Martin Curley

Just a thought

I thought that I would write fiction
That we each had a book in our soul
I've got lots of memories buzzing around
But a story I just haven't found.

I thought that my letters were good
I could make people smile with my prose
Writing a letter versus writing a book
It's not what I thought I suppose

I thought I could write of my exploits
Over a fifty-year span
Continuing into my dotage
Starting when my life began

But I can't and I shan't.
I thought that I did but I don't
I gave it a try but gave up with a sigh.
I thought that I would but I won't!

Ruth Hughes

Dive into a poem

The Echo Man

Tears are running down a single face
Turned away from the sun never seeing light
Darkness is never a comfort
Sound diverges under the Echo Man

His song grips your heart in ice
Supplanting your voice with whispers
Disfiguring your face and eyes wide
Delirium is the tonic of the Echo Man

Lurching over the hellscape
Barely aware of reality which bends and blurs
Thoughts so black and evil
Your mind belongs to the Echo Man

Night is eternal and rage takes form
With wings that beat in time with your heart
Feasting on nothing substantial
Such is the price of the Echo Man

Limbs heavy with every breath
Poison going in and life trickling out
Eager to please his every whim
Obey the commands of the Echo Man

The world is fire and ash
The living tremble in fear at his spawn
Days of brimstone and burning flesh
This is the world of the Echo Man

Christopher Trezise

Black on White

Just now a bird gave me the evil eye.
I never was one to notice such things,
My own were more on skirts that flapped than wings.

Carry on, carrion, black and beady,
Rendered by charcoal and the artist's skill.
Outstare me if you like, I'm not so weedy,
Wishing me dead, you have no power to kill.

I notice creatures of the earth and sky
Solely pinned by art, or smashed and left to die.

Don't think you'll sit that perch so proud for ever
Each dog has its day, each crow its night.
A cat could leave you bone and bloody feather.
Down, down you come, for malice is not might.

David G Bailey

Dive into a poem

The Book Club

The first Thursday is here once more
Bookclub members at the door
In shuffles Barbara looking grim
Julie whispers, 'Can I come in?'

Jill curls up nice and neat
while the others find their seat
Next we start on tea and chat
Talk about this and that

The Royal Family, Breaking News
Cost of living, price of booze
Talking of which, let's pour the wine
It's only Pinot but it tastes fine!

Down to business let's take a look
And discuss the merits of the book
A tale of smugglers, Frenchmen's Creek
Says Jill, 'We were in Cornwall just last week.'

Barbara brightens up a tad,
'We're having a pirate party for our lad.'
Come on you lot stay on task
'Who was your favourite character?' I ask

'Is that the time, I've got to go,
work tomorrow, I'm sure you know.'
One by one they fade away
The review must wait for another day!

Susan McCranor

I Wuz Robbed!

And when, in glints of gold, I think I see
That distant hint of wealth which should be mine,
I have to bring to mind that reasons be
Which separate me from that cash sublime.
So here I sit, a humble Homo Sap
And sap may well be right, today's mot juste.
To him who has my funds I doff my cap,
My fortune's gone for ever and I'm bust!
'But why?' I hear you ask, and sounding vexed,
'Why does this sad misfortune haunt your mind?'
Let me explain, as no doubt you're perplexed,
My wealthy forbear died, left all behind.
Of his two sons, the elder took the lot,
And I'm descended from the younger clot!

Philip Gregge

Dive into a poem

A boy named Bill (love)

On one hand Billy tattooed the word love, on the other the word hate.

Well I never did know my dad and mom
So I guess I'll just call 'em May and Tom
A GI Joe and a pretty little country girl.
He left her when I was minus zero
So you can't call him my boyhood hero
Even if that weren't exactly how it did unfurl.

Just one step away from the workhouse herself,
I see May couldn't be left on the shelf,
She only did just what she had to do.
I can't say if they were really kin,
Uncle John Aunt June who took me in,
But they was both good people, decent through and through.

Now I grew up smart but I grew up mean,
Bully as a boy and worse as a teen,
Fight men screw girls was all I had in mind.
But I really knew that it was all a bluff
Deep down I was never good enough
Else why would everyone leave me behind.

Then I got my luckiest break in life
In a bar of course where I met my wife,
My wife to be at least as she was then.
They warned me off cos she had a kid,
But the smartest thing that I ever did,
Was to marry that sweet girl and her little Ben.

So happy when she said that she'd be mine,
But no idea of how to walk that line,
She sure deserved a better man than me.
Even when our little Jack came along,
I still had trouble telling right from wrong
There's none so blind as them that will not see.

Dive into a poem

She opened up my eyes all right
When I came home one stormy night,
Standing there waiting right behind that door.
She said, 'Boy you better shape up fast
Else this night'll likely be your last,
You can turn and run right back to your Russian hoor.'
Yeah, that's what she told me.

Now she raked her heels right down my shin
That was just so I'd bring down my chin
She stuck on the nut to mash my lips real bad.
I raised my hands but I would never hit her,
And she was screaming 'You chicken shit you're
A no good husband but an even worser dad.'

'Why don't you piss off like your old man did?
I've done it before I can raise your kid
Without one single speck of help from you.'
I thought she was laughing but soon saw not,
Her face was a mess of tears and snot,
I never had less idea of what to do.

Still I grabbed her tight and behind her head
I whispered and scooted Jack back to bed,
Praying he'd think it was just some awful dream.
To her I didn't say much at all,
I wasn't proud but I wouldn't crawl
Nor string myself up like I might from the nearest beam.

So I made her a vow by the wind and rain
That she'd never have to bust my snout again,
If she'd take me in out of that filthy weather.
Now I still don't claim to be the best of men,
As she only reminds me a time or ten,
But at least I know we'll both grow old together.

And I hope we'll go together to the Lord above,
Where at last I can show her a better love
Eternity won't be long enough for me and her.
When at last I've kissed my mother's face,
I might even holler down to the other place,
'Hey Tom – let me say thank you, Sir.'

David G Bailey

Dive into a poem

A boy named Bill (hate)

On one hand Billy tattooed the word love, on the other the word hate.

Now my daddy was just a GI Joe
Or at least my Uncle John told me so
I couldn't ask my mum and looks like I never will.
He left her when I was less than zero
That chickenshit yankee local hero
Gave me his name, said they used to call him Wild Bill.

Might have even been true, but I'll be blunt,
I reckon he was just one lying ****
And still I tried to be my father's son.
Don't know John and June was really kin,
But they was good enough to take me in
Then must have wished a million times they hadn't done.

Not once did they throw back in my face,
When I brought home only shame and disgrace,
Wild Bill, King Billy were my playground names.
When I hit my teens things could only get worse
For all June would cry and Johnny curse,
School done for me once I sent it up in flames.

Now it was Mildenhall in mid-July
On the US base I was kinda high,
A local girl, I don't recall her name.
I asked her nice if she wanted to dance,
I really thought I had a chance,
Till a Yankee voice said, 'Buddy what's your game?'

Well I never did find out who he was,
I tell you it hardly mattered much because
It weren't about him nor the girl who caught my eye.
They may have called me Billy the Kid,
But in time of trouble I never hid
'I'll show you game all right, you little shite, if you wanna try.'

Dive into a poem

I gave him my best shot across the jaw.
Maybe he weren't coming back for more.
I leave him there and things take off on another course.
Tho' I never come near to takin' his life,
I did notch his face with a Stanley knife
When they sent me down they blamed me for not showing no remorse.

You know that I've done time since then,
You could say I grew up in the pen
And not just because that's where I turned twenty-one
I couldn't be trusted out on parole
And I had a few jobs but mainly dole,
Getting paid for the things I had and hadn't done.

John could only ask me why
Guess he was sicker than I was seeing Aunt June cry
Had to leave them good folks behind and be on my way.
One more time I had to beg their help again
Look after my own boy David Wayne,
Don't be like me son, every night I pray.

Course when he was born I gave it a go
Playing happy families with him and Jo,
Didn't last long though we both gave it our best shot.
The child wasn't planned you ****ing kidding?
And she wasn't a girl set to do my bidding
Some men can live with that, and some will not.

I'm a reader, had the leisure
While serving time at Her Majesty's pleasure,
I know there's a tide in the affairs of men.
So I'm a rigging myself up a jury mast,
A rope, a chair, a kick and I'm past,
The fret of another stretch of five to ten.
And I won't be crying for my mum at my final twitch,
But still kicking and a cursing 'Dad, you son of a bitch.'

David G Bailey

Dive into a poem

Well, Tuck your Frock

Well, tuck your frock into your knickers then.
You've nothing you can swim in, once again!
You said you'd bring your bathers by yourself.
I bet they're hanging on the bathroom shelf.
We can't go back a second time today.
Not to our digs. The landlady did say.
And only paddle in the shallow part,
I've no more dry clothes with me. Look, sweetheart.

What now? Oh, no. that frock is soaking wet.
This seaside break's a treat I won't forget.
You shouldn't have gone as far as to your knees.
Just get it off; I'll dry it in the breeze.

You had a donkey ride two days ago,
The dodgems, and The Punch and Judy show.
We're well beyond our budget for today.
We're on a beach. Why can't you go and play?
You've got your bucket, spade and sea and sand.
And if the sun comes out, you might get tanned.
This seaside entertainment is all free.
Just do not build your castle near the sea.

I said the tide was coming in quite fast.
You should have known, built there, it wouldn't last.
Don't answer me in such a mardy tone,
Just leave me for a minute on my own.
And don't get lost this time. Don't go too far.
Remember where I am – by Joe Blog's Bar.

Dive into a poem

Oh dear, what's up? That's such a sulky pout.
The tide's come in. But now the sun is out!
I didn't know the bars were all called that.
You're back at last. You'll need to get your hat.
You left it with your bathers. Should've guessed.
Sometimes, you know, you can be such a pest.
Stop grizzling and we'll share a bag of chips.
That's better, with a smile upon your lips.
I've got a nice surprise for you in store,
Your just reward: at least you're not a bore.
I've paid a whole half-crown to get in here,
Come on, Christine, I'll race you down the pier.

Chris Rowe

Dive into a poem

Balletic Experience

I went to the Ballet, not just to see;
I went to the Ballet in order to be –
part of the set-up, part of the show,
primped, primed and costumed and ready to go.

I was one of the knitters setting the scene
sitting on hay bale on village green,
and rubbing shoulders with the King and Queen
(now can you believe that!)

It started some weeks back when I got through the post,
the usual junk mail, along with a host
of advertised shows at the Warwick Arts,
and there was an advert offering a part,
(to a woman of age; that's me)

The ballet wasn't of the usual sort,
with tutus and leggings and folk that cavort,
accompanied by music ever so classical –
Oh no no no, this was more of a spectacle fantastical.

There were dancing sheep, children a frolicking,
hobby horses, hula hoops, rocking horse and slides,
people that lived and others that died.
(Well that's life isn't it?)

There was mesmeration in every scene,
gold dust and stardust and magic between –
every gyration and every prance
that the acrobatic troupe gave to their dance;
and there was I being a part
of this wonderful show at the Warwick Arts.

I didn't even act as I sat on the bale
with a smile on my face, like a dog with two tails.
Three oldies (us knitters) had our own dressing room,
furnished with tea, coffee and biscuits – all of which we consumed.
We were spoilt rotten, cosseted, and looked after;
the dressing room rang with chatter and laughter
(and we'd just only met!)

Dive into a poem

The staff always knocked as they came to our door saying "15 minutes"
or "nearly time",
then on we went ready to shine –
but the sparkle we added was but a fraction
of this amazing, stupendous *Rumplestiltskin* attraction.

Ann Cooper

Dive into a poem

Don't put me in a box

Don't put me in a box.
I don't want to be like you,
or anyone else.
I want to be me.

Don't put me in a box,
criticise me for being different,
talk about me behind my back,
make assumptions, try to 'help.'

Don't put me in a box
just because you think you know best
what's good for me,
how I should be.

Stay in your box.
Leave me be
to live my life, happy, free.
You are you and I am me.

Rosemary Marks

Dive into a poem

Iron Horse

The misty road and the iron horse
It trod in times of yore
Belching smoke and cinders
It shook us to the core

The mighty engine snorting
Its flanks as black as coal
The rails beneath are trembling
This machine had got a soul

From Rugby on to Leamington
Through bridges and past roads
The countryside just rolled by
The engineer at the controls

Now those days are over
The rails long since gone
The iron horse gone to pasture
When the railway was withdrawn

Silence returned to the rail bed
Nature claimed back her own
Abandoned to scenic beauty
When it became quite overgrown

Then when hope was lost
And a passage was no more
Sustrans and the greenway
And a new pathway was restored.

Patrick Garrett

Dive into a poem

Railroad Blues

The poem was inspired by this picture taken by Martin Curley.

It was coming on Christmas,
I'm travelling in some vehicle
Going station to station and I can't speak the lingo
Clickety click clickety clack
From Plaza de Espana to Santo Domingo

No-one is talking to each other,
Most are on their phones
Gabriella closes her eyes by the window,
All her data has been spent
And Martina sends her last text
Her phone is down to eleven percent

The only guy in the carriage is Edwin Flagg
Can't use his phone because it's been hacked
Carmen is listening to Taylor Swift
Everyone being careful not to make eye contact

Dive into a poem

Angelou grips the hand-rail, she's all alone again
She and Daniel just couldn't make amends
But you're never really alone with an iPhone
She still has thirty-two Facebook friends

All aboard the night-train
No-one is smiling, no-one has the wind in their sales
No-one is looking at anyone else
Everyone's just tryin' hard to stay on the rails

Everyone has somewhere to go
From Salamanca to Bangkok
This is the new generation
These are the new girls on the block

Another day in the big city
No-one looks at ease
It's the same all over the world
Every day is a mighty tight squeeze

Two girls are staring at the floor
One looks like she's in distress
Climb aboard for a free-ride on the ghost train
This isn't the Marrakesh Express

This isn't the new skank
Hoping everything will work out fine
They have hopes and dreams and ambitions
Which they will all carry to the end of the line

Martin Curley

Dive into a poem

My final sonnet

Spenser wrote them in the Faerie Queen,
Shakespeare showed us how to get them right,
Meredith stretched the lines out to sixteen,
and I'm still trying far into the night.
My first attempt was on the signs of spring.
It wasn't half as good as one of Will's.
I tried all day but could not write a thing.
I couldn't find a rhyme for daffodils.
By midnight I was tearing out my hair,
by 3 a.m. I wished I was in bed.
My sonnet wasn't going anywhere,
and I was going out of my poor head.
I won't mention all the wine I drank.
In future I shall keep my verses blank.

Wendy Goulstone

Graham

Do you remember Graham?
You know who I mean,
That awkward looking gangly boy
We all made fun of at school.
He stood a bit awkwardly, and got
Knocked about by us and our 'accidental' collisions;
Wasn't it a laugh?
Do you remember how we stole his briefcase
and threw it round the classroom?
And how he couldn't speak very clearly or easily,
Especially those German words and French phrases,
And how he could never manage the high jump in PE
or pass the ball in rugby.
He wasn't one of us, probably one of them.
Sure, he wasn't bad at science
But who cares about that if you're not
One of the lads?
And didn't he join that nerdy astronomy society that met at lunchtimes
Talking about stars and planets and all that shit,
Oh and he was in the local paper meeting Patrick Moore
when he visited.
Poor old Graham, he never was very popular
And didn't we make him know it?
Didn't we make his life misery because he was a bit different?
Strange thing is, I googled him the other day
During my teabreak at the call centre.
Turns out he's working for NASA now,
Some sort of space project.
Leading guy in his field, they say.
Who cares? Not me.
Graham...
What a weirdo.

John Howes

Dive into a poem

She Knows Her Place

She wanted to speak but they wouldn't allow her
People were lying in the corridors of power
Cometh the woman cometh the hour
She wanted to speak but they wouldn't allow her
They waste every second every minute every hour
They're not hungry for truth they're hungry for power
She wanted to speak but they wouldn't allow her
People were lying in the corridors of power

Martin Curley

Stillborn

Precious lamb, you never knew the world,
No battles won, no flag unfurled,
No career, no treasures gained,
No courting made, no love proclaimed,
No generations, no parent's joy,
No kiss of hope, for girl or boy,
No brand new day, no sunrise warming,
No fading star, no twilight falling,
No grieving time, no pain nor sorrow,
No looking back, no fear for tomorrow,
To flower, in a better place,
In God's heav'n, in His embrace,
No toil nor strife, no change diurnal,
To know His face, His love eternal.

Brian Haynes

Play with Me

A muffled "Mama!"
and I'm jolted up off the sofa, running
      (for the fourth time tonight)
to your room, pausing to listen outside,
like a doe's raised tail,
teasing open the door in case you are asleep and the cry was actually the downstairs neighbour, crooning another Euro-pop tune,
or one of the phantom child cries that haunt me when we are apart.
Opening the door tentatively
      (perhaps you ARE asleep, and I can finish a cup of liquid gold
      (hot tea) - once you were born, this became the grail)
but I see you
sat up in bed, bedcovers askew and your hair crumpled around your little accusatory face, scrunched up and wet with tears.
Pushing the door open I quickly rush to your side, murmuring soothing words and kindness.
Your eyes close as you sink, tiny body relaxing, into the comfort of your safe place
      (how strange that is me; that I am this for another soul)
as soft cotton brushes against baby skin, and we hold each other, warm, safe.

"Bad dream?"
You nod and clutch my hand and I'm struck by how tiny your warm little grip is. I pat you.
"Mama, stay."
I lie down with you but my spirit is in the other room, brush in hand, crouching down to stir the blue-green emulsion and grinning at the sight of the Caribbean sea right here in this metal tin, about to collide with the dining room then
I'm back with you
staring at the shadows on the opposite wall
and the stacked bookcases that need to be better balanced, and books re-organised
      (immediately, an itch to fix them begins)
but ignoring it
I try to be in the 'moment'
and you're more valuable than the list of things I still need to do.

Dive into a poem

I didn't remember that earlier when you said, *"Play with me, Mama,"*
holding out Snakes & Ladders,
I missed that chance
and I shooed you away as I was cooking
but I decide I can still be a Good Mum.
I begin to sing *Curly Up, Safe and Snug*
and it's a ballad, being sung in the most even way I can muster, whilst lying down
> (let's face it, it is an evening performance for the neighbours, and
> I should try to do it well for them, because)

you're already asleep.

I look at you and smile and
I'm struck again by the wonder of your little nose, your sweet, miniature chin,
your tiny feet are my lifeblood and your face is the reason I keep going.
> (Being with you reminds me of when Verita's mum came into
> school to bake cookies over 30 years ago and
>> how the aroma of warm butter crumbled together with flour and
>> sugar spread through the room before we even took the biscuits
>> out of the oven, and
>> it was the most comforting, homey,
>>> epitome-of-Motherhood-smell, which I've never forgotten.)

Once, my life was wide and tall and then you arrived, and it included you,
now, joyously, my life is you and some peripheral rubbish.

I fall asleep in the warm cosiness of my unexpected safe place and then, groggy, I'm up
but, resolve renewed, I shift focus to doing things just for you
and scrub
at your little desk with a soft blue cloth
to rub away
the pencil and crayon scribbles and
brush away
so many spongey rubber fragments from your energetic erasing.
Earlier by this desk, you had asked *"Play with me, Mama,"*
clutching a colouring book in your podgy little hands, but
I missed that chance
as I shooed you away from the hoover, I recall, as
I'm filing away a suite of pencils, felt-tip pens and thick bright crayons
into your stationery holder next to the ceramic unicorn we painted "together"
> (you splashed paint in hideous shades of brown whilst I mostly

Dive into a poem

    looked at my phone)
and look at that,
you having a little desk, full of fun and stickers,
    (across from my big desk, overflowing with post, forms and bills).

I snag against your laundry drying on the airer as I move to the kitchen,
Step over yet-to-be-put-away delivered groceries
(a convenience tax)
still thinking of how many times you asked *"Play with me"* today and how
I missed those chances.
I wash your little dishes by hand, trying to hack through the Amazonia that is my to do list
    (but I am using a nail clipper, so I'll be a while).
Perhaps, by the time I reach the end of it,
you'll have shed your baby years and be grown
and I'll realise, I have missed those as well.

A.A.Malik

Dive into a poem

Love

After all this time I love you
We were one I always knew
From the first moment I saw you
My affection grew and grew

We've laughed and cried together
In good times and in bad
Even when tragedy happened
For the good times we were glad

And now the years are passing
And our memories can bring a tear
Our bond as strong as ever
All through those very many years

After all this time I love you
We were one I always knew
From the first moment I saw you
My love just grew and grew

Patrick Garrett

Dive into a poem

As Ash Wednesday Falls on Valentine's Day 2024

Of life, of love, of death, we are
all from the same earth,
I contemplate this as they murmur in the church
Ashes to ashes, dust to dust
All of us rise as a crocus to the light,
and from that we're born, out of dust, surely more?
And I say, is that all?
Is that all that we are? I cry no!
Love proves we are more, we have thought,
we have fight, we would give our last breath
for the ones we love most,
Ashes to ashes, dust to dust, a cross on my forehead,
a reminder for us – not to linger, consider
the flowers in the field, how they bloom and wither,
each counted, each precious, each fragrant and new,
But my love is for you,
all for you, all for you
in the shadows of candles, the quiet, the hush,
in the whisper of prayers there are wishes, desires,
because life is for loving and love is forgiving
and when the wind turns we are gone.

Theresa Le Flem 2024

Faith

The tightrope walker walked the rope
High above the tide
The thousands watching wildly cheered
When he reached the other side

"Now I do the walk again,"
He told the watching throng,
"But this time with a wheelbarrow
That I shall push along

And also I shall mask my eyes
A blindfold I shall wear
Across the canyon I shall walk
Whilst into darkness stare."

The crowds went wild they clapped non stop
Some even stamped their feet
"Now hands up those who have the faith
This walk I can complete?"

A hundred thousand hands shot up
Their faith so strong and clear
So sure were they of his success
They gave another cheer

"I'm glad you have such faith," he said,
"Or I'd be at a loss
For now I want a volunteer
For me to push across."

A hundred thousand hands shot down
Not one remained on high
They bowed their heads for now no one
Could look him in the eye

"I thought as much," the walker mused,
"Your faith is small and narrow
For anyone whose faith is real
Would climb into my barrow

Dive into a poem

For faith is more than just belief
Faith is part of living
Faith takes risks, faith has cost
Faith involves self-giving."

Raymond Brown

Dive into a poem

Music Lover

If music be the food of love play on my heart strings,
tap a syncopated rhythm on my feet,
twang a tingly toccata
while we sing a sweet two-parta
as we do the light fandango to the beat.
Write a madrigal to croon to my left eyebrow,
dance the conga up my leg with finger tips,
could you strum a little bolder
that sweet nocturne on my shoulder,
play a moonlight serenade upon my lips.
Glide a grand glissando down my backbone,
vibrate a wild vibrato with your charms,
nothing would be finer if you plucked a G sharp minor
while conducting a concerto in my arms.

Wendy Goulstone

Dive into a poem

Musical Memories

Music of my childhood
Music of my youth
Whenever I hear it now
I wonder at the truth
behind some of those lyrics
What did they all mean
I wish I'd seen a picture
of Hawkwind's *Silver Machine*
I wish Marc could have told me
if he ever knew
what exactly was this thing
called a Metal Guru
And Lindisfarne, I wonder
in your musical rhyme
What made you think Fog on the Tyne
was completely yours, not mine
I wish I'd listened to Candi
when she said *Young Hearts Run Free*
Or gone to find the *Starman*
Bowie said was watching me
But I stayed safe in my bedroom
with Wizard and Alice too
Daily finding ways to
shock my poor parents anew
Now they are just memories
but I still listen in
and maybe have a little dance
when I feel like reminiscing

Rosemary Marks

Dive into a poem

Desert Island Disc

It was the early sixties when I saw her standing there
Both of us just fourteen years
We shared a love so rare

Sunday nights were magic, I spent them at her home
Her parents kept low profile
And left us all alone

We listened to the music, the Beatles were our choice
They sang the songs of joyful youth
And gave our love its voice

We twisted and shouted
We loved love me do
We shared all our loving
And I held her hand

Then one day it all ended, deep sadness had its say
Our Sunday nights were over
And I longed for yesterday

Now to my desert island what record would I bring?
Let it be the Beatles
To remind me as they sing

To remind me of those Sunday nights when magic filled the air
And once again through mist of time
To see her standing there

Raymond Brown

Dive into a poem

Silver Swan

When as a child I had the chance
to join a class, learn how to dance.
How I did scoff. To dance indeed!
I would much rather sit and read.
So while my friends all jumped and ran,
kicked a ball, cycled, and swam,
I'd settle in a cosy nook
and lose myself inside a book.

Life moved on. Along came hubby,
children and pets all constantly grubby.
Keeping house and dashing around,
my feet hardly ever touched the ground.
My books lay neglected, no time to read.
There were jobs to do, people to feed,
while working for money to pay our way.
Life was a chore, all work, not much play.

One day after watching *Riverdance*,
my daughter decided she'd like a chance
to jig and reel and diddly dee.
And that was perfectly fine by me,
because by now I was regretting
not learning pointes and pirouetting.
Feeling old and stiff and out of kilter,
I wished I could be a little bit fitter.

The years rolled on and so did I.
Reading and writing and painting the sky,
shopping, cleaning, arranging flowers,
retirement brought so many spare hours.
A stroll round the block, a slow walk in the park,
life was so quiet, no longer a lark.
Is this how it will be for the rest of my days?
I wished I could spend time in livelier ways.

Dive into a poem

Then my son met and married the lovely Hollie,
who thought, in her wisdom that it would be jolly
to set up a group to teach ladies to dance.
Come on, Mummy Rose she said, take a chance.
And I thought, well, what have I got to lose,
so I bought myself some ballet shoes.
And now, Plié, Glissé, Rond de jambe
can you believe it! I'm a Silver Swan!

And...
At this please do feel free to clap...
On Tuesdays I do tap!!

Rosemary Marks

Left to say

What is there left to say concerning love?
Too many songs and poems have been written–
Some claim the source of love is heav'n above
When they find the one who leaves them smitten.
I might sit down and pen a wistful tune
And sing it to my darling late one night.
We'll gaze up there and dream under the moon,
Romantic declarations seem so right.
But spare a thought for Jack or Jo or Jane
Alone, without, forlorn, beside themselves,
They won't be walking down some snowy lane
But drinking soup from supermarket shelves.
Their lives are lived in rooms too dark to tell,
Like prison cells, their solitary hell.

John Howes

Dive into a poem

The Last Sonnet

Should I compare thee to a summer's day,
No similarity e're would I find.
Our climate degraded in ev'ry way,
Halcyon days have been left far behind.
Once we knew temperate times so benign,
Cool soothing evenings to sit and savour,
Soft nights when in restful sleep we'd recline,
Each fresh morning bestowed as a favour.
Such days sacrificed as temperatures surged,
Fierce howling winds, destruction increasing,
Tempest and deluge, our lands are submerged,
Oceans rising and shorelines receding.

So now, as our world succumbs to the flames,
No longer the question; Who bears the blame?

Steve Redshaw

Dive into a poem

Joyce Elizabeth

Joined not at birth, but at your end I was
Observer, server, through your failing years.
You sometimes did complain, and you had cause,
Careless in my youth, heedless of your fears
Even when the cause of them, a mother's tears.

Ever giving all to me, me only,
Love and feelings, not just pounds and pennies,
In return I left you often lonely.
Zealous yet to save me from my idiocies,
And how did I return what flowed from you,
Beyond the meagre money subsidies?
Except it's not in coin the debt was due.
The words, the kindness, caring, where were they?
Hard to admit, but lacking I must say.

David G Bailey

Dive into a poem

A sonnet for Queen Bess

Master Shakespeare, as the Queen's royal fool,
I beg for your help, Sire, on bended knee.
I am asked to scribe, but have not the school.
Yet how do I deny the suitor's plea?

What more need you, than sing, dance and be gay?
Authorship, need you not, to please the Queen.
I must pen a love note, poem or play;
A sonnet will do, if you scribe the scene.

What man asks a fool, is he friend or foe?
Tis a secret, yet it slips from my tongue.
Young Earl Southampton, Sire, Queen Bess's beau,
Then a sonnet I shall pen. Fool begone!

Shall I compare thee to a summer's day?
Nay, Will, not verses old, new rhymes I pray.

Madalyn Morgan

Heaven-sent

As I walked out one mid-summer morning,
With a light step and a song in my heart,
The long-hid sun was already shining,
I vowed that day that we would never part.
Cascades of ripe apples hung on the bough,
The gambolling lambs were now fully grown.
Summer is surely less lovely than thou,
So many shared pleasures, prior unknown.
But our impatient lives came a'calling,
Our fleeting season of love had to end.
Society's mores saw our world falling,
I am destined ever to call you 'friend'.
Today I give thanks for the time that we spent,
And know that you, my dear, were heaven-sent.

Simon Parker

Dive into a poem

Howling at the Moon

Most nights we'd walk Nick down Robb's Lane,
Nan making cocoa for us home again.
One time, while waiting for the pup to pee,
George looked up at the moon then down at me.

'They'll tell us if it's really cheese up there,
Them Yanks with all their fancy gear.
Man on the moon – who'd have dreamt it, Jim?'
(That never was my name to anyone but him).

Thirteen years old, to me 'space race'
Meant nothing but the look on Grandad's face.
'You know it's really something new,
We'll all be going in a year or two.'

But not before he died, five years back now.
We buried him, my nan lives on somehow.
I had to take old Nick to James and Blore,
The vets, she couldn't cope with him no more.

I can't say why, but I won't let
Our boy Jim have a dog as yet.
He haunts me for one. 'When, Dad, when?'
'When man walks on the moon again.'

David G Bailey

How about She Loves You, by the Bard?

Yet still bemoan'st thou thine unhappy state,
Thinking, thou dotard, she affect'st thee not.
Thou standest self-exiled at heaven's gate
Thinking but of thyself alone, God wot.
But yesterday saw I thy lady fair,
And thou art in her thoughts both day and night.
She sorroweth at thine absence, full of care,
And grievously with her tears did thee indict.
But thou may'st this distressed state forfend
With words of true contrition and regret.
Loss will be gain, thou can'st thy fate amend
And thus repay thy self-created debt.

Love's alchemy is best revealed in this –
That all can be redeemed with one sweet kiss.

Chris Stanley. Sorry Will.

Dive into a poem

The Food of Love

Shall I compare you to a piece of cake?
I think of you with every passing hour.
A cuddle, kiss and touch with you I'll bake
And trust our romance will not fade or sour.

Within the oven the gateau rises,
Moist and light with spice and sugary things,
Until the deep belly ache surprises,
The complexion turns green, the stomach stings.

Alas, I see this metaphoric sponge
Is only half-baked and sinks like a stone.
Into the depths my heart does plunge.
You've left me again; now I'm all alone.

Out of the pan our romance you did shove.
As the cookie crumbles, so does your love.

Fran Neatherway

Dive into a poem

Yet Again You Dodged

Yet again you dodged the twenty-ninth of February
And now there's no point in me waiting for next Leap Day
For you, there's no more indulgences in your sad rakery
Yet again you dodged the twenty-ninth of February
For you are no longer in hospital or mortuary
Your atoms are free, and flying far away
Yet again you dodged the twenty-ninth of February
And now there's no point in me waiting for next Leap Day

EE Blythe

Dive into a poem

It's not that late

Cold needles prick her eyes and sting her cheeks.
Her clothes stick to her like a second skin.
Through thick black clouds the watery moon peeks,
then hides. And darkness shrouds the street again.
Against the biting wind she rushes home.
The park gates loom. The path seems menacing.
A short cut if she dare while all alone.
She hesitates then makes her decision.
It's not that late. It should be safe.
She moves forward through the rain.

The park is dark, the lighting scarce and dim.
She hurries on. But wait, what can she hear?
The trees reach out, their branches long and thin.
With pounding heart she hurries on in fear.
She stops a moment, looks. There's nothing there.
Berates herself, yet still she senses him.
With trembling knees and resonating blood
in her ears, she resolves to carry on.
It's not that late. It should be safe.
She turns and runs through the rain.

She can hear him now, running after her.
Distant houses promise sanctuary.
She can feel him now. His breath is on her neck.
She cries out. As she stumbles she can see
a bedroom light go on, then off again.
Winking. The chase is over. Finally.
He grabs her round the throat. A silent scream.
The knife is cold. He cuts her, painlessly.
It's not that late. It should be safe.
She surrenders in the rain.

Rosemary Marks

Dive into a poem

Voices from the darkness

Voices from the darkness
We never seemed to hear
Rumours that all's not well
Of ignorance and fear

Though they lie to our faces
But we shrug it must be so
We really don't believe it
Then we just go with the flow

Now the curtain rises
The performance was an act
We say we knew it all along
The purpose now a fact

Those voices from the darkness
We could hear them all along
Just choosing to ignore them
Once again we were so wrong?

Patrick Garrett

Dive into a poem

Where Did It Go Wrong?

Standing on the edge of Seven Sisters
She was motionless, on her right foot was a blister.
Staring out to sea
But didn't feel free
On her own, no sign of her "Mr".

Thinking of climbing down to the beach
She could swim out into the English Channel as this was within reach
Whether from above on the cliff
Or below on the beach with the help of a skiff
Both methods would do the job, actions you couldn't teach.

Looking around, all she could see was blue sky, clouds and greenery.
A visual delight of a scenery
Free from no other living soul
Nevertheless unsure of her goal
Not even the sound of any machinery.

What was she to do? Why was she here?
What had happened in her life that she was shedding a tear?
Seven Sisters – was this the right location?
What was her intended creation?
Perhaps to cause her "Mr" inescapable fear.

East Sussex filled her with lots of thoughts
Mostly happy ones, but the last one was painful and fraught.
Coming to terms with being single… again!
A bit older, wiser and slimmer, with the perception of vain
It wouldn't be long before she is caught.

Moving into her new home and excited about the next chapter in her life
She was adamant that she didn't want any more strife.
Very keen in her search for a husband
A man she could walk alongside hand in hand
For all she wanted to be was a loving wife.

Dive into a poem

She heard a noise outside in the garden but from next door.
Sneaking up on tip toe she popped her head over the fence and across the paved floor
There he was... the most gorgeous, mature and cuddly neighbour!
Tempting eye candy for her to savour!
Quietly to herself, she voiced an internal roar.

But that was three years ago when they met
And things had changed dramatically causing her upset.
Had he let her down?
Enough that she considered a drown?
Where did it go wrong as their wedding in Autumn was set?

Neleh Yartel

Hope

She came when I needed her most.
I didn't seek her
I didn't expect her
I didn't foresee her

She came.
Like sunrise at the dawn
Like light piercing the darkness
Like the birth of a new star

"There were signs all around," she said.
"Signs which told of my coming
Signs which promised my arrival
Signs which pointed to me."

She came.
Through the form of other people
In the guise of the Word made flesh
She came.
And said her name was hope.

Raymond Brown

Dive into a poem

I Miss You So

A Villanelle

Summoned towards the moon and stars so high,
A life too short is what he had been thrown.
He did not hear when I bid him goodbye.

I begged, why him? then gazed unto the sky,
Dark truth to bear he must journey alone,
Summoned towards the moon and stars so high.

We pledged our love, something money can't buy,
The vows we made, were they made on my own?
He did not hear when I bid him goodbye.

Dreams in my head will be our bond our tie,
Knowing he leaves just our names cast in stone,
Summoned towards the moon and stars so high.

When time is nigh unclip those wings and fly,
Deep wounds sever my heart, it throbs, I groan,
He did not hear when I bid him goodbye.

Beside my skin is where my man should lie,
His warmth has gone, and his spirit has flown,
Summoned towards the moon and stars so high,
He did not hear when I bid him goodbye.

Caroline Lucy

One Kiss

That one kiss
That was all it took
That first kiss
That told us everything

We never really needed words
We knew each other's heart
We knew each other's mind
We hardly ever needed words

That one kiss
That I still feel now
That one kiss
That fused us for ever

EE Blythe

To All the Lovers I Never Had

You could not see
I loved you from afar
your laugh, your smile
your handsome looks
but thank you now
for not acknowledging
my breaking heart.
At somewhat over
threescore years and ten
and meeting you again
I thank my lucky stars
that we remained apart.

Wendy Goulstone

Dive into a poem

The Poppy

The thunder of the guns, the flashes in the sky
soldiers in the trenches watched as comrades died
It was truly hell on Earth, nowhere for to hide
This was the war to end all wars the politicians lied.

Four years and four months the carnage carried on
Seeing things that none should ever see, it was the devil's spawn
The filth, the stench and corpses lay there so forlorn
How could god have turned his back, let this thing carry on.

Then the war was over, the thunder was no more
The killing fields were silent, earth filled with blood and gore
The ghosts of fallen soldiers far from homeland shores
Never again to see their loved ones, go knocking on their doors.

The world at last it took a sigh and many tears were shed
Falling on the ravaged earth, where the young men bled
This land of desolation, a place so full of dread
Is now awash with flowers with Poppies oh so red.

Patrick Garrett

Blown Up

I bought an inflatable sheep, ta ra,
It came with a guarantee,
I needed the bleater
'Cos real ones are fleeter
And run much faster than me.

But the salesman surely fleeced me, ta ra,
I was up for money each day,
For I hadn't a clue
An inflatable ewe,
Must be fed on inflatable hay.

Next was a blow up paddock, ta ra,
With an air-filled miniature dam,
And then I discover,
My pneumatic lover's
Run off with a helium ram.

It's put me off sheep for life, ta ra,
Even made me allergic to wool,
But life's better now
I've moved in with a cow,
Who loves me 'cos I'm full of bull.

Geoff Hill

Dive into a poem

Tess and the Mayor

At one thirty the Mayor of Casterbridge went home
There was no-one there he was all alone
At half past two there was a knock on the door
And the Mayor of Casterbridge was alone no-more

Tess of the D'Urbervilles had come to call
She hung her coat and brolly in the hall
She was such a pretty site for the Mayor to see
They went into the parlour and had cake and tea

This is very nice just us two
Yes said Tess I've always been fond of you
True, two's company three is a crowd
One more person shouldn't be allowed

You're not expecting anyone else this afternoon?
Not at all he said, but he spoke too soon
Just then there was a pounding on the door
And a voice said let me in, it's Jude the Obscure

So against their wishes they let him in
And he scoffed the last piece of cake in the tin
The mayor put on a dress and a purple wig
Tess got on the table and did a jig

I think I should leave said Jude dis-hearted
Nonsense, this party's just getting started
And look outside it's started to rain
Tess went to the fridge and bought back Champagne

The mayor jumped on Tess till she was squashed
They'd drank so much they were completely sloshed
Then they made love under the mayor's cloak
And when they finished they had a smoke

Would you like to have a go said Tess to Jude
She was smiling 'cause she'd just been screwed
But the prude Jude thought it rude to be so crude
So he just sat there in a bad mood

Dive into a poem

Hey Mayor said Tess if you think you're able
I can fetch the donkey from the stable
Let's take this party up a notch
You can do the donkey and Jude can watch

Oh bless my soul said Jude, you're both insane
I must leave at once I can't remain
I shall never come here again he vowed
And fled far from the madding crowd

Martin Curley

Dive into a poem

Eighty Years On

We'd always find the boxing tent at village fairs.
He needn't fret, I'd always tag along.
I mind them still, across these eighty years.

A break from landwork, and domestic cares
(He hit her sometimes, though he knew it wrong)
We'd always find the boxing tent at village fairs.

My pleas were no more use than mother's tears,
The blows I took as well, till I grew strong.
I mind them still, across these eighty years.

With friends he'd put the gloves on in their lairs,
Closed doors, for nights of sparring, drunken song.
We'd always find the boxing tent at village fairs.

Yet who would tote me tenderly upstairs,
His bone-deep smell of baccy, sweaty pong.
I mind them still, across these eighty years.

Those tents now serve up other wares,
The fights impromptu, not announced by gong.
We'd always find the boxing tent at village fairs.
I mind them still, across these eighty years.

David G Bailey

Dive into a poem

The Deafening Sound of Silence

On a solid chair he sits,
Staring, lost in his own thoughts.
On a solid chair she sits,
Busily thumbing through her messages.
On a solid table there sits a solitary pink top bottle.
It stands between them.
On the floor there lies
His rucksack with the broken zip,
His solitary white top bottle spilling from the crack in it.
On the floor there lies
Her ballet plimsole, petite and delicate,
Her stockingless foot tapping on the edge of it.
Their possessions lie between them.
Unblinking, he bends, wraps his fingers
Around his bottle and takes a swig.
Message sent, she wraps her fingers
Around her bottle and draws it to her lips.
The silence is deafening between them.

Caroline Lucy

Dive into a poem

Born and quickly forgotten

A blinding flash of promised life; the gates open into a tyrannical world.

Turbulent beginnings: blood, screaming, and masks.
A babe is dragged to the cold embrace of an unloving world.

Slender, track-marked arms hold the wonder of life.
Lovelessly, thinking only of relentless needs, wants, and desires.

A defenceless party favour withdrawn from its mother's womb,
poisoned, craving love and care.
The gift of precious life diminished to resentment and despair.

The mask of a doting mother quickly cast aside.
The needle penetrates her, sweet brown relief permeating her milk,
soothing the baby's cries.

Unwanted and disregarded like rubbish on the floor,
unworthy of a mother's love, the festering of self-loathing takes hold.

Life's relentless jackhammer breaks what is innocent and pure,
stealing the promise from what could have been a bright burning star.

Dean Speed

Dive into a poem

My Perfect Wardrobe

I do like shopping for clothes,
Though there are some colours I loathe.

For instance, I've never liked grey
Reminds me of my old school uniform in which we used to play

Every piece of clothing nowadays comes in black
Including comfy cotton knickers folded neatly in a pack

I hardly wear any clothes in white
As they are difficult to keep clean and bright

Brown doesn't suit me but can suit others
Later on in the year as part of the autumn colours

What should I wear today? Depends on my mood
Vibrant colours are my favourite to help me feel good

As I open my perfect wardrobe painted in plum
A variety of many colours stop me from looking glum

Yellow, orange and even purple and red
Looking at what to wear, styling it out in my head

If it is sunny outside perhaps a multi-colour dress
A maxi or shorter length as long as I impress

Or should I instead wear a skirt?
Feminine and fashionable and still able to flirt!

I have other items and footwear in navy and burgundy
Dark colours as a base matched with my bright personality!

My colourful collection of clothes contained like a strobe
Time to close the doors on my perfect wardrobe.

Neleh Yartel

Dive into a poem

The Cramp

(Tune: *The Lark in the Morning*)

Oh the cramp in the night-time it strikes you in your bed;
It seizes on yer leg until you wish that you were dead.
And like the jolly birdie you rise up in the air,
Then you fall back on the bed with the sweat all in your hair.

Oh the cramp in the morning it gets you in your hips
And you rise up in the air with a scream upon yer lips.
You wake the jolly neighbours who curse you with their shouts
And when the fight is o'er you get three months or thereabouts.

Oh the cramp in the daytime is not so very bad,
But it gets to you in places that you didn't know you had.
There's shouting and there's screaming and then you come crashing
down, Which gets you funny looks in the middle of the town.

Oh the cramp in the evening it gets you everywhere
And you jiggle and you wriggle as you sit upon your chair.
And then you stand and jump and shout and make a wild display
Which leaves you quite embarrassed in the middle of the play.

And when your time is over and they lay you in your grave
The coffin starts to jump and shout, yer voice begins to rave.
And just as they begin to flee with all their might and main,
They'll dimly hear the cry, "Oh no! The cramp has struck again!"

Philip Gregge

Dive into a poem

Onomato-alphabet

Aaah
 Blip
  Cluck
   Drip
    Eeyore
     Flutter
      Giggle
       Hooray
        Itchy
         Judder
          Kapow
           Lisp
            Moo
             Nee-nah
              Oscillate
               Parp
                Quiet
                 Rampage
                  Snip
                   Thrum
                    Unzip
                     Vroom
                      Woof
                       Xxxx
                        Yippee
                         Zzzz

John Howes

Dive into a poem

Making Plans

He said he had a great vision
That would get us all excited
Small-minded and long in the tooth
His vision is very short-sighted

We've heard all this before
We don't need all that again
The last time he rocked up
He left a litany of pain

Stood in a bar in a cloud of fag smoke
Puffing away and beer he's quaffing
A relentless man with no filter
That boffin would look better in a coffin

He's stood seven times in different places
To try and get himself elected
But the people spoke and spoke again
And seven times he was rejected

Like a bug-eyed monster from the deep
Well under par and over-rated
Everything he says from his pulpit
Sounds like it's computer generated

He's bad and he's back
Pointing out the things you lack
He's like a nightmare in the middle of the day
With his nonsense of bric-a-brac

'I'm quite good at bringing people together'
And that's a direct quote
He'll appear chummy and friendly
And then he'll go for your throat

Who will rid us of this turbulent beast
Like a fairy-tale he makes life Grimm
There he goes again
Will we ever see the back of him

Dive into a poem

So he's off to Clacton on Sea
He will not be denied
We're all going on a summer holiday
Oh he does like to be by the sea-side

Martin Curley, General Election 2024

Dive into a poem

Dry My Tears

Oh Israel, what have you done?
And you Christians?
You Muslims?
You Buddhists?
You Hindus?
You Atheists?
You Believers?
You Non-Believers?
You People?
You Sons of God, Jehovah, Yahweh, Shiva, All There Is?
What have you done to your Home?
What have you done to your Palace?
What have you done to your Playground?
What have you done to the Gift I gave you
And why?
To bathe in non-existent wealth?
To build towers to nowhere?
To live from the proceeds of destruction?
To foment war and destroy the Peace of others for imagined slights?
To take power and control over that which does not belong to you?
No, not yours because it's mine, ours!
Everything belongs to us all,
From the tiniest microorganism to the Heavens and beyond.
None of this is yours to take or destroy,
Not a single breath is yours to smother,
Nothing is yours and yours alone,
Nothing!
How dare you destroy my property, my garden, my life!
Who gave you that permission?
Not me nor any I know.
Oh, you decided it was your right did you?
It's your Birthright, your historic possession, your Revenge?
For what? For nothing!
Revenge is never best served at any temperature,
Revenge is best never served at all.
It's not too late, there's still time,
Time to turn around and repair the damage,
Restore what was to what is,
Create New with Love and Compassion,
In cooperation with your Neighbours,
All of them,

Dive into a poem

For they are also You as I am You.
To continue down your current path only leads to your annihilation,
Turn back before you cross that line,
Before the Chasm opens up behind you,
Before your existence is snuffed out
Like a candle in the darkness.
Desist!
Do not resist!
Allow the Love of your God,
Your Source,
Your All There Is,
Of Yourselves,
To flow,
Freely,
Abundantly,
And allow me to dry my tears.

Jeremy Sadler-Scott

Dive into a poem

I don't like Mondays

No more Monday mornings
No more gloomy, grey-skies-dawning Mondays
No more grungy, tawdry, crotchety Mondays
No more dingy, mirky, frowsy Mondays
No more what-time-is-the-electrician-coming Mondays
No more check-the-bank-account, rate-of-interest Mondays
No more cold cup of tea, change-the-bedspread Mondays
No more inside washing, machine-noisy Mondays
No more soggy lawn, cat-turd garden Mondays
No more Wimbledon-washout, Test Match rained off Mondays
No more suspicious pain, neck headache Mondays
No more politician interviews, only-one-poll-that-counts Mondays
No more Rishi Sunak, Nigel Farage Mondays
No more Booker-prizewinning-novel-to-read-by-Thursday Mondays
No more don't-talk-to-me, I'm in a bad mood Mondays
No more stop-walking-in-front-of-the-telly Mondays
No more empty-the-dishwasher, hide-the-broken-glass Mondays
No more did-you-watch-the-football Mondays
No more far–too-cheerful radio presenter Mondays
No more why-has-he-parked-his-huge-van-outside-our-house Mondays
No more dog-crap-on-the-pavement Mondays
No more can't-get-the-Wordle-today Mondays
No more newsflashes-about-absolutely-nothing Mondays
No more atheism, this-is-all-there-is Mondays
Just, just, go away Mondays - please.

Start the week on a Tuesday instead.

John Howes

Dive into a poem

Why Do I Bother?

Why do I bother feeding that bloomin' cat?
He turns his nose up, meowing 'I'm not eating that!'
He'd rather have what I've got, he'd rather I spent more
on gourmet food in a tin so small it'd fit into his paw,
and costs a bloomin' fortune. He thinks I'm daft. I'm not!
As my old mum would say, he can be grateful for what he's got.

Why do I bother buying special food for that dog?
He'll eat absolutely anything, he's a proper bloomin' hog.
The other day I caught him with his nose stuck in the bin.
He'd tipped it over on one side and then he tucked right in
to all the scraps and rubbish, spread them all across the floor.
By the time I'd cleaned and sorted it, my poor old back was sore.

Why do I bother cooking dinner for my old man?
He'd rather have a pint of beer straight out of the can.
He'd rather spend his days between the bookies and the pub,
while I'm stuck in the kitchen cooking his bloomin' grub.
I should just leave the lot of them; I'm fed up with this slog.
Go have some fun, leave a note, 'Your dinner's in the dog.'

Why did I bother taking my own advice?
I looked online, found a hotel that seemed really quite nice.
Until I got there and the rooms were manky as could be.
The food was just revolting and I couldn't see the sea
because of all the rain. And the wind pinched my favourite hat.
I very soon decided I'd had quite enough of that.

I was amazed when I got back, the dog was pleased to see me.
The cat even sat on my lap and made pin holes in my knee.
And when the old man came home, said thank God that I was back,
that he'd try harder in future, well, I thought my face would crack.
I told him how I was surprised and grateful that he'd offered.
But I prefer to do it all myself and I'd rather he didn't bother.

Rosemary Marks

Gluttony

She'd just finished eating her way
through everything on the table – all homemade.
In those days people invited you round for high-tea;
sandwiches, sausage rolls, cheese scones, almond tarts,
lemon meringue and queen cakes.
She'd always had a sweet tooth – couldn't get enough.
There was something extra special
when someone else did all the cooking.
She wanted to be seen to appreciate it,
besides, she didn't want to miss out...
it was a compulsion really
and at times she couldn't stop herself
from doing a second round, so to speak.

Even though the band of her skirt
was biting into the extended flesh of her waist,
and causing great discomfort, still she couldn't stop.
It pained her both physically and emotionally
to leave the table while there was food still left on it,
beckoning, asking to be taken.
As she flopped back uncomfortably into the armchair,
distended from her table pilgrimage,
she couldn't help but notice
the opened box of candied fruits on the coffee table nearby.
Automatically she stretched out her hand.

Ann Cooper

Dive into a poem

The Winner

Create your own label, vary the landscape,
Vines winding their way to the sky, alpine climbs,
Switchbacks along the dark dusty lane.
Joggers, walkers, wobblers in the way.
Where's your bell? Where's your pavement?
Ruthless headwind shadowing the clouds.
Dismiss that trickle of competitive urges and
Suck in your silent surroundings.
Give a two-finger wave to the rain
And utter the words 'I'm the winner',
While stealing that thirst-quenching pint
From its well-deserved place on the podium.

Caroline Lucy

Dive into a poem

The Satnav

He came in late again from work,
thrust pink carnations in my hand
bought from the garage down the road.
He really is the greatest berk
to think that I don't understand
that this is how he gets his kicks
alone with his dominatrix
switched on to sultry mode.

He made excuses, said he had a cold,
I'll sleep in the spare room, he said,
but unconcerned I dimmed the light
put on my negligee, the gold,
perfumed my hair, slid into bed,
then softly so he would not hear
whispered in my true love's ear
and slept with Siri all the night.

Wendy Goulstone

Winner of *The Oldie* Competition 195, December 2015

A Sonnet

A sonnet was the task of the Café Writers,
I felt constrained by word frighteners!
Too clever for me by half,
So let's have a laugh!
I shall rebel,
Not to write a sonnet, a simple poem,
A short poem, *I'll* show 'em.

What is a sonnet?
Not pretty as a fancy bonnet
A sonnet is poetic
Devised in the Sicilian city of Palermo
The brief is not in *my* manifesto.

A sonnet is of one stanza
Some sort of extravaganza
It's a 14 line poem to write,
I tried long into the night.
A strict rhyming scheme,
Something of the like *I've* never seen.

Let them be clever
It's a task beyond *my* comprehension
And not my endeavour
To compile a sonnet
No, *I'll* watch *Wallace and Gromit*.

Kate A Harris

Dive into a poem

A Non-Sonnet

I've often wished that I could write a sonn-
et. A bright idea arrives and then is
gone. It is so hard to squeeze the sounds in
line, get the rhythm right and then the rhyme.
Sonnets are poems highly organised.
If I succeed, what if I'm plagiarised?
It's maybe not a very likely sto-
ry, but my toil's no gift for other's glo-
ry. A break should just now have here occurred,
A rhyme-scheme change, or moving a mere word.
So let me set it down all plain and clear.
Don't try your copying tricks on this one here:
You'll only show yourself as insincere.
You'll just not get away with it, no fear!

Chris Rowe

Dive into a poem

Dive into a poem

Where did the loving go?

I don't know where the loving went.
it seemed so real that I was caught
not knowing it was only lent.

The woods and valleys I frequent
in search of love that can't be bought.
I don't know where the loving went.

I wrote a letter. It was sent
with kisses plenty. I was fraught
and feared that all his love was spent.

If I've done wrong I now repent.
We never argued, never fought.
My words were always kindly mean.

I tried his house. He was absent.
My searching always comes to nought
He'd left and paid the final rent.

He didn't ask for my consent.
From this lesson I've been taught.
I know now where the loving went.
It was not given only lent.

Wendy Goulstone

First time

I think it was a Friday morning
When she said it.
I was alone in the office
Looking out of the window
onto a grey car park.
The sun wasn't shining;
Her voice was barely a whisper
on the telephone,
Hardly hearable yet definite,
Unexpected yet welcome.
After preamble about the day ahead
And how we might meet,
She said, for the first time, 'I love you.'
I'd heard it before from others
Even sincerely spoken
But nothing prepared me for the wonder
Of those three words
From that sweet person—
Heart-felt, honest, brave.
God knows I didn't deserve it.
In the corniest of ripostes, I came back with
'I love you, too.'
Not original and not the first time I'd used the line either
But I hadn't meant it before,
And now I understood,
Really understood
What life was all about.

John Howes

Dive into a poem

No New Beginnings

Don't tell me to start again
I haven't got the strength
I'm too old
Too ill
So low

Don't tell me there'll be someone new
I haven't got the heart
Or the time
Too low
So lost

Don't tell me I must carry on
I haven't got the need
Let me go
Too lost
So dead

EE Blythe

A Lonely Soul

Dear Darlings, I thought I would write and say
I hope you're well and happy. I miss you.
Can you guess what your old Nan did today?
I went to town and bought myself a book.
Before you ask, it's not just any tome,
it's been my favourite since I was a child.
It would be so nice if one day really soon
we can set off on the quest, a fearless bunch.
We'll battle with a dragon, we won't stop
until we've won. Well, maybe just for lunch.
If you ever come to stay.

I was around the same age you are now,
when I opened the first page and met new friends.
A wizard, dwarves, small folk with hairy feet,
they took me all the way deep underground;
no place for a feint hearted child like me.
There we met a feral being. I was enthralled
by his large feet and bulging, big round eyes,
his exaggerated S'sss, his slimy skin.
And in some cruel part of my childish mind,
I thought of poor old Joe who lived next door,
and likened him to Gollum.

Each day old Joe would place a rickety chair,
behind his broken gate and there he'd sit.
Mouth slimy with spittle, face creased with age,
straggly grey hair sparse on his shiny head.
The busy, bustling world would pass him by
while he tried to entertain folk with his wit.
My mum would stop and pass the time with him,
I would stare, entranced by his toothless smile.
His open mouth a chasm. What lay within?
He frightened me, I did not want to know.
And yet I was beguiled.

Dive into a poem

I'd cling to Mum, then try to sidle past.
He'd beckon, 'Would you like a sweet, my dear?'
I'd shake my head and I would quickly run
to the sanctuary of my own back door.
Safely inside I'd open up my book
and lose myself in a time long ago.
I'd chuckle to myself when Gollum said,
'Teeth! Teeth! My preciousss; but we only has six!'
At least he had six more than old man Joe.
In my naivety I did not see.
He was a lonely soul.

If only I had known how fast the years
speed by. You blink and suddenly they're gone.
If only I had been able to hold
your mummies and your daddies a while longer.
But they had to grow, to leave. That's how life is,
the young must fly, the old must soldier on.
I cannot tell you just how much I miss
them. And my parents, siblings, all long gone.
There wasn't time to think, or time to be
in this race of life we are all enrolled in.
And which nobody will win

It's only now that I am old and grey,
my own eyes ancient and my teeth long gone.
That I have time to sit and ruminate
on how often we decide others are wrong.
We laugh at those who are different to ourselves.
We criticise, we rush, we want, we take.
My darlings, please, don't make the same mistakes.
Don't pass judgement on that which you don't know,
and even if familiar, then be kind.
Cruelty and compassion quite simply are,
Only a state of mind.

Dive into a poem

So my darlings until we meet again,
be kind, be true, work hard, be sure to play.
Don't be in such a rush to be grown up,
that will come to you suddenly one day.
Never judge. Do not let yourselves be judged.
No-one's accountable for you, but you.
Before all others makes sure that you love,
yourselves. To yourself you must always be true.
Then everything will fall right into place
and maybe if you ask you'll be allowed.
To visit me for a while.

Rosemary Marks

Dive into a poem

Conversation with a Shaving Mirror

The bathroom mirror in my mother's home
Saw my face yesterday again through shaving foam.
One side reflects a bigger face than t'other,
For make-up I suppose, so seldom used by Mother.
The angle of its face can be adjusted,
To suit your height but now the hinge is busted.
It hangs its head and catches me chest high,
That is, about the level of my mother's eye.

It wasn't always so.
Before I moved away and father died,
We kept its chin up, head up as in pride.
But now it's irremediably low.
I couldn't fix it, never even tried,
Just finished shaving, turned my head away and sighed.

David G Bailey

Dive into a poem

Designer Shoes

And another thing, stop eating all that chocolate
Stop returning all my calls
Take stock of your situation
Tear down your load-bearing walls

Cancel all your subscriptions
Do unto yourself as you would to another
Lower all your expectations
Never raise your voice to your mother

Never try to be the first in-line
Re-examine all your faults
Accept nothing less than the second best
Learn to play the Black Hawk Waltz

Try and steer clear of vampires
Never put your foot in a bear-trap
Always greet a tiger with a smile
Spend some time popping bubble wrap

Ignore people who say they're aliens
They're really not one of us
Quit putting sugar in your tea
Don't swear out loud on the bus

Cut your own hair with this thing
Wear clothes that have gone out of style
Never polish your shoes when they're wet
Read a good book once in a while

Clear the snow from your neighbours driveway
Go and see *The Mikado* at the Savoy
Try and cut down on your screen-time
Hey, Father, can you help an old altar boy?

Save your empty jam-jars
Re-cycle your knicker elastic
Learn to draw cartoons
The Brown Dirt Cowboy and *Captain Fantastic*

Dive into a poem

Wear an old jumper around the house
But always step out in style
Have a lie down in a darkened room
And think about infinity for a while

If you pay heed to all in this creed
You could really make the grade
Never keep off the grass
But stay away from the deadly nightshade

Come and step into the parlour
Hang up your coat and shake off the snow
Come and sit by the fireside
Mama turn your lamp down low

Buy a copy of the Big Issue
Help old ladies across the street
Always have ink in your pen
And you'll always end up on your feet

Always try and see the best in folk
Never do anything to raise a red flag
Never patronise children, you were young once
Pack up your troubles in your old kit bag

I gave up my job as a theoretical physicist
And failed to make it as a pop star
But everything is tickety boo now
If you want me I'll be in the bar

Do what thou wilt shall be the whole of the law
Keep me in mind, whether near or far
Thank you, toda, Shukran, merci
If you want me I'll be in the bar

Martin Curley

Dive into a poem

Pandemic 2020

What can be said about these very strange times
When being together is almost a crime
When visiting friends could bring them swift death
The streets are all empty so others have breath

We cannot shake hands, like times of yore
Or even a hug, case we might just give more
Don't get any nearer than six feet be sure
Because for the ailment, there still is no cure

We can't say goodbye to friends who have passed on
Or even get married because of the deadly spawn
The shops are all closed so we all stay at home
Can't even go wandering in the Park for a roam

Once we warned children when they went out
Now their shouting at us, it's dangerous they spout
Gatherings of two are deemed as a crowd
Police they will tell us we could end up in a shroud

But these times will pass, as sure as times do
When we are all pleased just to catch flu
A vaccine they'll find and we'll breathe once again
Go out in the evening to visit our friends.

Families united who have been too long apart
Friends coming round and their stories impart
Those very strange times that we have all shared
When again we go out without being scared.

Patrick Garrett

Dive into a poem

Lockdown Dreamer

I look out from my window
And view the world outside
For me a long forbidden place
From which I still must hide

I glimpse at passing buses
I hear a distant train
I yearn to be aboard them
And travel once again

Then I see a distant bird
Wheeling upon high
Exultant in his freedom
Playing with the sky

Oh that I could be that bird
And flee my lockdown place
Oh that I could fly away
And with the clouds might race

I'd fly and fly and never stop
Until the earth had gone
I would kiss the passing stars
And journey on and on

Raymond Brown

Dive into a poem

Dad's Old Shed

Hidden behind the apple trees at the bottom of the garden,
with an old tin roof that played a tune when it rained;
and rough planks that enticed small hands
then threw out splinters to split the skin;
and with gaps in its walls that let the winter winds whistle in,
sat Dad's rickety old shed.
His pride and joy.

A treasure trove of 'things'. Old, past their best. Kept, 'Just in case.'
Which were guarded by spiders and the occasional mouse.
The mouse trap was on the top shelf, at the back,
much to our mum's chagrin.
Dad couldn't bear to use it, said killing anything was a sin.
So he left it to next doors cat
to do the dirty work.

A meeting place to drink beer and chew the cud. A sanctuary
when the in-laws came to call.
A forbidden den when children got the chance,
a secret smoking place for all.
Dad's old shed was everything and more.
Such happy times, such fun. Times long gone that I often yearn for.
Someone else's refuge now.

Rosemary Marks

Dive into a poem

Anthony Edwards

Although I cannot claim I knew you well
Nor would, yet proud to know you as I did.
The father of my dearest friend, Nigel,
Had nothing but respect and love for Dad.
Our paths will cross no more down here below
Nor perhaps above (though we can always pray)
Yet God will speed you to His arms, I know.

Every best wish in grief I send your way,
Dear Margaret, with Paul and Anne-Marie,
Who bear the loss of Tony every day,
And much-loved grandkids, friends and family,
Respect and love from all, your legacy.
Death is no final step, your faith hold true
So Nigel open-armed will welcome you.

David G Bailey

Dive into a poem

The Day That Never Was

It was going to be limeade green
His was going to be ecru, or cream
It was going to be sometime in the future
When we'd both lost some weight, and got fit

There was no rush to make it happen
We'd conceded it was what we both wanted
We would play around with the formalities
Even though we'd both said 'Never again!'

But it never happened – not deemed urgent
Hardly ever mentioned, except now and again
As a jest, or a jibe when at odds – And in time
Put off, in hopes of healthier days

So the limeade green frock that never was
Was metaphorically hung in the wardrobe
And next to it in an identical cover
Hung the invisible cream three piece suit

EE Blythe

Dive into a poem

Autumn Has Arrived

Days are getting shorter as the nights draw in,
Looking at the trees and bushes as their leaves change their colourin',
Some fall to the ground,
Walk on them for that "crunch" sound,
While others blow in the wind rustlin'.

Autumn has arrived with its vivid statement,
A visual blaze of colours right here as summer went,
Time to cosy up inside,
Hot chocolate or minestrone soup, you decide,
Either sends out rich, soothing and comforting scent.

The month of September is just the start,
Still some sunny days as on the weather chart,
Autumnal fruits are ripe to pick,
Plums, apples and blackberries some people nick,
They've come prepared with their big wooden greenish cart!

Early morning greetings appear with a layer of fog,
In the countryside as opposed to city and town smog,
A sight similar to cotton wool,
Could the fog be hiding a ghoul?
Arriving in time for the Halloween shopping slog!

Children's outfits of purple, orange and black,
Different characters and creatures walk the streets in a pack,
Knock, knock, who's there?
Uninvited guests demanding sweets in the flavour of pear,
Just give them a bag in the hope they don't come back!

Gone has October as we flow into November,
Bonfire Night coming up to remember,
Lots of displays about,
Would be fab to be get out,
For an evening, watching the fireworks and ember.

How gorgeous and spectacular the bright colours against the night sky,
Visitors "ooh-ing" and "aaaahs..." as they sigh,
On one side is the bonfire,
Keeping the visitors drier,
From the light spray of rain as it trickles down and multiply.

Dive into a poem

November is also a time for reflection,
Remembrance Sunday every year is tradition,
Advent in December cometh,
Carol singers and choirs sing and hummeth,
As Autumn departs into Winter in its transition.

Neleh Yartel

Dive into a poem

Dad Two

In memory of Rob

So where do I start with this tale of me and you,
The man who would become my dad - number 2,
In the beginning the enemy, who should not be named,
Don't know why you're a villain, it was never explained,
Forever in my orbit, like the dark of the moon,
Not realising that would all change and would be happening soon,

For the standard family structure of 2+2,
Was never something I had really knew,
My parents of life, always together,
For me that dream did not last forever,

And so from out of the gloom this man does appear,
Not a monster or villain or someone to fear,
A head full of curls and a beard on his chin,
A twinkle in the eye and a cheeky old grin,

We have things in common, bikes, art and even more,
I remember discussing them while sat on the floor.
As the years slowly passed I got to know you,
The man that became my dad number 2,

But then things all changed, the stroke took it all,
Leaving the shell of this man standing tall,
The face was the same but the man I knew gone,
The quirks and mannerism, guitar playing none,

And then all of sudden you were off and away,
I hoped that you'd come back, I hoped that you'd stay,

For years you went back to the dark of the moon,
The man in my orbit, out of sight in the gloom
I was angry you left us, I couldn't see why,
You wouldn't let us help you, you wouldn't let us try,

Then the day of the phone call, the sum of all fears,
The end at last looming, my eyes filled with tears,
I had so much to tell you, I hoped that you knew,
You loved me like a son, and as a dad I loved you.
Red Wellies

Dive into a poem

Colourful Vibes

Calypso colours all bright and gaudy.
Religious colours that shout, "Oh Lordy."
Colours that sizzle like the morning sun –
That makes the adorned just want to have fun.
Rainbow hues of magnificent spectrum,
Make you happy when you bedeck them.
Zingy yellows and tongue tingling limes,
Vibrant oranges that make this verse rhyme,
The stand-to-attention of pillar box red,
And a purple that stretches from A to Z.
I'll dress me in colours that tell you I'm bold,
And make people smile when me they behold

Ann Cooper

Dive into a poem

Waiting for Juliet

Earth
Newly
Turned for her.
A place of sleep.
Dark, cold, and lonely.
But not for long she waits.
When the sun shines bright again,
Through a tunnel long and narrow,
Her lover, Romeo, takes her hand.
Young again, well again, happy again.

Madalyn Morgan

Dive into a poem

Autumn Girl

I'm an Autumn Girl
Just look at me
Kicking up the leaves
In the golden sunshine
I'm an Autumn Girl
Just watch me go
Walking in the wind
Got a grin on my face

I'm an Autumn Girl
Look at my colour
Climbing in the trees
Camouflaged by nature
I'm an Autumn Girl
In heart and soul
Not the Summer Girl
That I was meant to be

I'm an Autumn Girl
Just look at me
Kicking up the leaves
In the golden sunshine
I'm an Autumn Girl
Look at my colour
I'm an Autumn Girl
As I was meant to be

EE Blythe

Dive into a poem

Sharing the Load - Derwentwater

On the fringe of the lake
a crowd has gathered
to watch the show.

Two collies are bounding
on the shingle
waiting for the toss

and here it comes
ears prick, tails thrash,
heads up, and they're off

into the ripples
with a great splash
paws paddling like mad

and what happens next
is a wonder to behold
for this is no ordinary stick

this is a branch of huge dimensions
and these are no ordinary dogs.
The spectators are agog.

Each dog bites an end of the branch
and they bring it to shore,
working together in perfect harmony.
The audience applauds.

Wendy Goulstone

Bus journey

Here we are in the sun. On the bus
Journey just begun. Stopped outside
Royal Leamington Spa, why are we delayed?
Too early to proceed, quiet, few stops on the route.
Wow, bright sun burning, scorching my arm, by the window.

Cover up, lovely sun, we will be moving again, soon.
Time past, cappuccino cake is safe, good purchase,
Out of sun, on the floor. Now busy, about 30 people.
Many passengers on number 63 bus. Where's that mobile?
Whose is it? There's a mobile tune blaring out.

"Hello, it's Pat." "Oh hello, Sue. I'll see you in 20 minutes.
Are you alright? Yes, what? You've a cracked rib?
Oh dear how's your breathing? Oh, really?
Don't do much, need a rest.
It's my cholesterol, only slightly higher today."

"I go to see the doc again, Tuesday. I'm nearly there."
The noisy bus engine starts up again
Noisy, rattling, dangerous, something bumping at the rear.
Somebody pushed the bell, last minute.
We stop suddenly with a jumpy back pull.

The gears grate and change. Sun flashing,
Through the trees, dappling, flashing, hot,
Heat pouring through the closed window.
Other arm hot now, wearing purple fleece, long sleeves.
Protected. Bus soon zooms away from the sunlight.

"Still lovely, no clouds, too hot. Bye Sue." Older lady
Finished her conversation. Low hum of engine.
No 63, rumbling wheels. More rumbles due.
Rumble strips, reminiscent of Fairs that amuse.
Osteopaedic bones, roundabouts, dodgem all.

Now in Southam back amongst houses
Shade from brilliant sun for a while. Countryside.
That's the limit of hot, hot sun, nobody talks
Too noisy, rickety. Sheep and cattle grazing in fields.
Brown and cream Jacob sheep, White Short Horn cattle.

Dive into a poem

It's summer. There's the Polo Field. Any connection to Dallas?
I wonder, I doubt it. At last. In Leamington. A Business Conference
In Pump Rooms, Leamington, keen young man, promoting Polo,
With horses, not the sweets. I look up to see elegant chandeliers,
Cascading with crystals. "Look, modern, we have the same."

He, the young man, said. "Oh, incredulous really.
Yes," he continued, "we are having the same,
At the Manor House Hotel we're cleaning.
We had everything from a nearby dilapidated hotel,
Even chandeliers, architraves and an enormous mural.

"They daubed it front to back on a ceiling.
Not sure which, beautiful, boutique hotel
It's a 5* hotel. Somewhere, not sure where!"
"Time for me to disappear," I reply, "I've nattered on."
"Have a good day," he says. I wished him the same.

"Good luck selling your Polo days." I didn't say more.
There was a young lady, petite, pretty hair, long and blonde.
Back to his world of selling. Me, back to my world.
On this mode of transport, a bus, home to Rugby, Leamington
Via Southam. No talking, all single passengers. Off we go, good timing.

A young girl, short brown hair, green anorak,
Pinging, pushed the bell twice. Time to disembark.
Accompanies another girl, green parka, fake fur trim.
Off she goes, clutching her plastic bag of shopping.
Maybe visiting, off to work, late shift, who knows?

Those days gone for me. Bus headed for Draycote Water.
Faster, faster, driver's foot on accelerator, catching up with timetable.
Still sunny, hedges flashing by, slow for right turn.
It's Stockton, here we come. Ten percent gradient,
Downhill, narrow roads, very narrow. Vehicles obstruct our way.

Waiting. Soon move off and uneventful remainder of journey.
Bus halts in Rugby centre. I climb down the steps and off the bus...

Kate A. Harris

Dive into a poem

Oxford Thoughts

The enchanted dreaming city, beautiful and well
If it could tell its story what story it might tell

The noble Radcliffe Camera, regal in its magic
The solemn toll of Great Tom sounding deep and tragic

The drama of St. Mary's, standing on the High
Its old all-seeing spire pointing to the sky

The academic park serene beside the river
To strollers in high summer a peace it can deliver

The Bird and Baby pub where Narnia was born
Where Lewis and friend Tolkien chatted in the morn

The welcoming Sheldonian where honours are conferred
Where issues are debated with passion undeterred

The Memorial to Martyrs where Cranmer met his end
Where Latimer and Ridley their truth they did defend

The many ancient colleges reflecting English history
On foggy winter's evenings, beguiling in their mystery

Embracing generations of energetic youth
Sheltering the minds who wrestled here with truth

Oxford's silent story has so much more to say
A city always dreaming and dreaming still today

Raymond Brown

Dive into a poem

Transported or The Art of Sitting Still

The interior of the ambulance was like a flat.
You could live in it easily, a bed for one,
a couple of chairs, plenty of cupboards,
room for a table. A bit short of 'conveniences',
but that could be fixed with a bit of ingenuity.

When we arrived, the waiting room was packed.
'Is this the queue?' I asked, as my heart sank
to my boots. 'You'll be called,' she said,
and disappeared. Time 11.30am. I sat, and sat, and sat.
At last, a few preliminaries, temperature, oxygen level,
blood pressure off the top of that hotel in Dubai.

And again, I sat, and sat, and sat. At last
two of us were scooped up into wheelchairs,
given a half mile tour of the nether regions
of the hospital, and deposited in Minor Injuries.
We thought, great, at last. But no, we were beaten to it
by rows and rows of the bruised and battered,
where we sat and sat and sat.

At last, at *last*, 6.00pm to be exact, I was escorted
into a matchbox-sized consulting room, to be inspected
by the only doctor on duty that day. Young, handsome,
thorough. He cleaned up my face, wiped off the dirt
from the brick paving in the backyard, stuck plasters
on the worst bits, went through all the tests again,
and gasped at my blood pressure reading.
'It will take 10 days to heal,' he said, waving goodbye.

Wendy Goulstone

Dive into a poem

Bored and Lodging in UHCW*

I'm over the hurdle
      of Wordle

I'm losing my skill
      at Kill-
      er sudoku

The binary puzzle
      is friendly, then snarls.
      It needs a muzzle.

The anagrams are making
      my system eyes misty
No. that's not quight rite

I cross swords with crosswords
      and it's makinbg this in-patient
          Impatient
      and using too many cross words

My knitting's OK till I drop a stitch
      then it's a bitch

My ssight and my hearing
      are both disappearing

I'm bored and frustrated
      Life's balloon is deflated

Perhaps I should sleep, but then
      when I wake it'll happen all over again.

Jenny Hicks

*UHCW stands for University Hospitals Coventry and Warwickshire

Dive into a poem

Dive into a poem

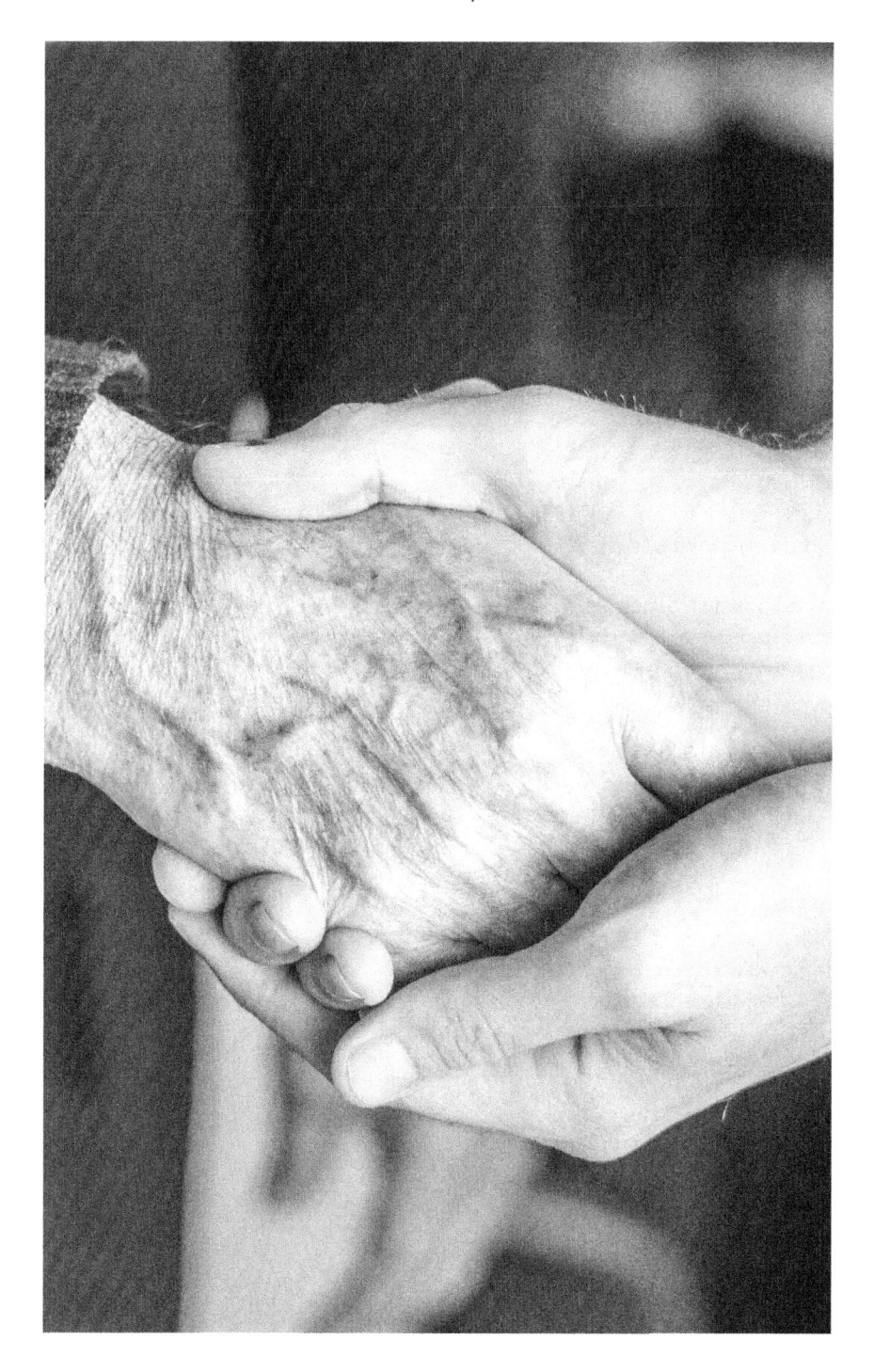

Dive into a poem

Old Age

I sat there thinking in my chair
Of the age I had become
My hair was grey, my eyes were dim
My youthful days long done

Inside me was a nagging fear
Of what the future held
Decline of body and of mind
Mortality it yelled

I protested at my ageing state
Bemoaned the curse of years
Against the loss of youthfulness
I mourned with silent tears

But then a story came to me
Of Noah from of old
He lived for some nine hundred years
Or so the story told

I thought about that story
And what it meant today
What did those ancient writers mean?
What did they try to say?

Suddenly I saw it
The veil began to lift
The ancient writers spread the word
That old age is a gift

A gift to be received with thanks
A gift beyond all measure
A gift with which to bless the world
A gift we're called to treasure

Raymond Brown

Now and Then

Things are different for kids today
No time to just go out and play
 Evenings and holidays, always clubs
Football, Tennis, Guides and Cubs

Looking back our days were long
Summer holidays went on and on
Go Karts made of box and plank
Rolling down a grassy bank

 Chased away from neighbours wall
Giggling girls play two ball
Making mud pies, flying kites
Riding on my brother's bike

Now, parties are not held at home
It's welcome to the pleasure dome!
A themed event with catered food
The whole class comes you can't be rude

All the games are fun but 'fair'
everyone's a winner there
All the guests will get a prize
That doesn't come as a surprise

 Health and Safety is a thing,
Gluten free for little Tim
Sofia is fussy and can be contrary
As for Raj he can't eat dairy

Harry mustn't drink the juice
One small sip he turns quite puce,
Lucy's airway will close right up
If she has a sniff of nut

We didn't give these things a thought
Mum just used what she had bought
Jelly, ice cream an iced sponge cake
Anything else that she could make

Dive into a poem

Because it was my brother and me
We could each invite three friends to tea
We played pass the parcel, musical chairs
One winner per game, it seemed quite fair.

Kids today, so cool with tech
But when the WiFi's down, Oh heck!
 Games to play and opponents to beat
And only virtual friends to meet

How different it was way back then
Splattering with a fountain pen
Telly broadcast in shades of grey
Talk of the playground the very next day

It's not all bad now, I must say
When my Grandson comes to stay
He eats my cakes, updates my phone
And today he let me fly his drone

Susan McCranor

Dive into a poem

The daydream

I daydream I'm a model on a photo shoot in Spain –
draped on bending palm tree as they shoot me frame by frame.
With my sprayed on gold bikini that reflects the sunlight's glare.
and half a fruit bowl's contents intertwined among my hair.
My nails and lips are lacquered in a flaming hot-house red
While my black mascaraed eyes whisper softly, "come to bed".
A hunky man in James Bond shorts is lying at my feet,
feeding me with truffles and exotic things to eat.
I hardly have to move at all as I'm powder puffed and preened,
massaged, manicured and sprayed with oil- it's every female's dream.
"For god's sake get that kettle on, I'm gagging for a drink."
The bubbles burst, my reverie gone, I'm at the kitchen sink.
His master's voice booms over the latest football scores
and I'm back inside my own domain, instead of distant shores.

Ann Cooper

Dive into a poem

Gremlins on the lines

Those little green men are at it again
zipped into their overalls
throwing spanners into the works.

That one there, up on the desk
In the stationmaster's office,
tearing timetables into shreds,
wastepaper baskets spilling
trains to nowhere onto the floor.
And that one, in the driver's seat,
unscrewing knobs and levers,
smashing digital panels to smithereens,
sabotaging all hope of escape.

There's another, swinging with one hand
from the bracket holding the clock,
him with the smirk, sending the fingers
spinning round the dial. And those,
disguised as passengers, pushing
their way to the edge of the platform
determined to be first on board any train
to anywhere so long as it's moving.

And all the while the Controllers quaff their wine
pat their fat stomachs and plan their next flight
to some far-flung luxury destination
miles away from the havoc they have created.

Wendy Goulstone

Written during the Railway Workers' industrial action in 2023.

Dive into a poem

The Pudding Club

A friendly little venue
An afternoon so good
Full of anticipation
For connoisseurs of pud

So many fine confections
Laid out upon the top
A mousse full of chocolate
And a meringue that was hot.

I took a tiny pink one
Full of raspberries and cream
A delicious slice of roulade
The taste it was supreme

The cupcakes looked attractive
Displayed upon the stand
Full of fruit and icing
Looking very grand

When asked, 'Which one's your favourite?'
I just couldn't tell a lie
The best one for me by far
was the banoffee pie!

The base it tasted gorgeous
With its crunchy biscuit crumb
While the banoffee toffee caramel
was creamy on my tongue

A charming place, The Cava
We'd never been before
Thank you for the invite.
We'll be back for sure

Susan McCranor

Dive into a poem

So Faithfully Superstitious

I love my superstitions
They keep me safe all day.
They make my life worth living
They protect me, work or play.

I've lots of superstitions,
I can hardly count them all.
They protect me everywhere I go,
They save from every fall.

Whene'er I see a magpie
An umbrella, a black cat
My superstitions help me.
Now what do you think of that?

When I'm afraid of ladders,
When I cross on the stairs,
I touch my very own piece of wood,
It drives away all cares.

I love my superstitions,
They make my life worthwhile.
And if you have some more for me
I'll take them, with a smile.

And when at last, I'm going,
And I'm taking my last breath,
I'll cross my fingers, touch some wood
And I'll be safe - in death.

Philip Gregge

Dive into a poem

Trains

The maintenance man has
left us some cream eggs. This
I overheard on the
10.50 from Eastbourne.

John Howes

Dive into a poem

Last Orders

You can't play dominoes or skittles, now, in the village pub.
The multi-punctured dartboard has vanished from the wall.
There's no more talk of harvesting, of milk yield or of lambing.
You won't see a local farmer there in muddy boots at all.

You can't buy a pint of bitter in a dimpled, old, glass tankard.
They don't serve fish and chips, tomato ketchup, mushy peas,
nor a bag of cheese and vinegar, ready-salted, smoky bacon,
nor bangers and mash in Yorkshire pud with onion gravy, please.

The walls have had a coating of dove-grey and eau de nil;
the tables have been sanded for that authentic rustic look
and the French chef in the kitchen stirs jus á l'orange for duck.
Portions here are miniscule, prices astronomically high.
With pub and shop and youth club gone, village life will die.

Wendy Goulstone

Dive into a poem

Shirley A Thorpe

Sorting snaps a promised winter project,
Hard to accept you gone by shortest day.
I have an ample fund to recollect,
Remembrances of good times all the way.
Long summer holidays beside the sea,
Elbow scraped, pell-mell hand-in-hand downhill.
You meant no harm, just ran too fast for me
A strong pace all your life, to match your will.

Those Christmases, through childhood and my youth
Henson House, home from home till turn of year.
Outrageous feasts, and fun, and farts in truth,
Remain the standard gold for festive cheer.
Plain-speaking, hard-drinking, no-nonsense Shirl,
Ever-loving, sore-missed, deep-loved dear girl.

David G Bailey

Rain

When is the rain going to stop?
I wish it would go far away.
Jump into puddles, hop, hop, hop.
When is the rain going to stop?
All that water - I need a mop.
More and more rain each single day.
When is the rain going to stop?
I wish it would go far away.

Fran Neatherway

Dive into a poem

Hail Caesar! The Battle Cry

They thundered, plundered, fought with grit,
Hail Caesar! And commence battle –
the cry.

Rome's generals raised ten thousand men.
They fought, were killed, raised ten again,
To die.

Lances thrown and horses falling
Swords are drawn, soldiers are mourning,
the dead.

Army strongholds now depleted.
Garrisons and legions wiped out.
Defeated.

A bloody, broken army.
Beaten, they enter the city.
But why?

No standard for them raised on high.
No celebration feast or toast,
Just lies.

Hail Caesar, the victory cry.
Hail Caesar the generals lie
To wives.

Thus, another battle ensues.
Justice for the dead, or your head
Caesar!

Madalyn Morgan

Worshiper

From above, Sunlight shines in a bright haze,
My eyes sting from its benevolent gaze,
Thinking if the light, meant to be hopeful,
Was the catalyst of my own downfall...
Of course not! How dare I think of such things,
The Sun, the watchful eye of all beings,
Saving us, obscuring evil from us,

But what if...

My head turns away from the light,
The day falls into night,
Its stare was so bright and blinding,
I fall into a spiral of wanting,
To escape, to be freed,
From the choke hold I'm held
in.

Alicja Kulczak

Dive into a poem

Easter Light

It was still dark that Easter morn
When Mary reached the tomb
Her world was lost
Her life had died
Consumed by fear and gloom

But then the dawn began to break
And she began to see
The man with her
Who called her name
Was one who'd been set free

Set free from death's cold icy grip
Set free from death's dread sting
The dawn was here
The sun was up
New life was on the wing

Mary left the garden tomb
With awe and hope and sight
For she had glimpsed
A deeper truth
Born of the Easter light.

Raymond Brown

Dive into a poem

We Always Look Up

We always look up when we pray
Or at least direct them upwards, don't we?
Whether sitting, standing, kneeling, head bowed, prostrate,
We send our prayers, petitions, cries for help, frustrations
And so much more besides
To God, Allah, All There Is, Source,
Or other specific Deities
Who we believe to be Up There,
Somewhere above and beyond us,
Out of reach, invisible, unfathomable.
Yet, where is Up when you live on a Globe?
If Up in the North is the same Up as in the South
And in the East, the West and all Points in between,
Where exactly is Up?
The futility of it is a conundrum
Far beyond our analytical thinking processes
And yet there is a simple answer which we already know.
It's been taught to us since childhood,
Regardless which Belief System is followed,
Or even none as can also be the case.
We have been told, taught and instructed from Pulpits and Mounts,
From Platforms and Caves,
That God, or whichever Deity or label used,
Is Love.
And what is closely associated with Love,
The very Home where it is always found?
The Heart.
Our Hearts.
All Hearts.
So, there is no Up to Pray to, Petition, Beseech,
There is only our Heart Within.
Love is the Answer, Love is Within,
We are the Oneness Within.

Jeremy Sadler-Scott

Maggie

A Ballad

It was a mid-summer's evening
She arrived in a storm.
Fists clenched tight she hammered the door.
Blazing eyes full of scorn.

Sheltered from the harsh storm with love,
Kept safe this treasured gift.
Maggie's beauty bound for trouble,
It was her time to drift.

Whisky pressed tight to her red lips,
A spliff within her hand.
She danced with the devil till dawn
Thinking herself so grand.

Fairies and mushrooms cast their spells.
Take this hand it is kind.
Come back to earth sweet child I beg,
Leave that devil behind.

Caroline Lucy

Wasted

I ended up chained to a lamppost
When we took a trip to the coast
Saturday we had a kebab, Sunday a roast
I ended up chained to a lamppost
By Monday I looked like a ghost
Tom and Dick drank loads but I drank the most
I ended up chained to a lamppost
When we took a trip to the coast

Martin Curley

The Clown

Every night I entertain
People cheer, people claim
That in the circus I'm the star
Spreading mirth both near and far

But when it comes to end of show
With makeup off my smile does go
For I'm the saddest man in town
A tearful, broken hearted clown

Raymond Brown

Dive into a poem

Silver!

An array of colours and shades to choose,
Which one or two should I use?

On the ceiling, on the walls and on the floors,
This colourful vision and taste will be mine, not yours.

Let's start with my ceiling,
And find a shade that will be appealing.

Nothing dark and nothing too light,
Must mix in a touch of colour with the white.

What colour or shade should I put on the walls?
Red? Yellow? Or orange? A vivid shade that calls.

For my feature wall and the contrast of my living room,
As the main two colours on their own will be enough gloom.

There is nothing wrong with a white and grey theme,
Correction - I've picked silver along with objects that gleam!

That's it! I'm having scarlet red for my contrast,
A feature wall in silver and white-ish ceiling together with create a modest blast!

On my floor, a silver coloured carpet and fluffy fur rug in scarlet red,
So soft and warm to lie on, I must not mistake this for my bed!

The next project will be my hallway,
As I walk in through my front door I want to see a pictorial display.

The same colour theme I think to follow through,
But instead of scarlet red, I will swap this for navy blue.

Neleh Yartel

Writing

I thought that I would write fiction
That we each had a book in our minds
I've got lots of memories buzzing around
But a story I just haven't found
I thought that my letters were good
I could make people smile with my prose
But writing a letter versus writing a book
Is not what I thought I suppose
I thought I would write of my exploits
Over a fifty-year span
Continuing into my dotage
From when. My life first began
But I can't and I shan't
I thought that I did but I don't
I gave it a try but gave up with a sigh
I thought that I would but I won't.

Ruth Hughes

Dive into a poem

Barnardo's poem

The Heat is on, my taxi awaits
July 19, a date in the diary
Scorching hot temperatures, lower 30s.
Who turned on the Heat?
It's not Italy, really too hot to bear.

My arrival in my Airbnb
All comforts, a long-awaited Retreat.
That's my Writing Retreat.
Isolation, no TV, no radio, writing, writing
Turn off the Heat it's time to think.
Morley is *the* hot place to be.

Chrissie, mentor, local to the old Barnardo's,
Close proximity, half a mile, just a blink away.
Title of my book may, will change again
'Life in a Barnardo's Home'
Three exciting days, writing, writing.
Hot, hot, the Heat is on.

Information, memories flow, my memories.
A walk to Morley Manor, once a Barnardo's Home,
Three long years, two as a student, one qualified.
A nursery nurse qualification. A result, amazing.
Success, reward for hard work and dedication.

Difficulties remembering 55 years before
Running to the Smalley Crossroads
Catch the 7.30am bus to Ilkeston
Change buses bound for Nottingham.
College, early, early, hurry.
It's early, mustn't miss the bus.

Down Memory Lane, up the Derby road
Children, children everywhere, playing happily.
Back in the 1960s.
Meeting contributors, generous, contributors,
St. Matthew's Church, coffee morning, Wednesday
Hot, hot on the old croquet lawn, talking, and no croquet

Dive into a poem

Several ladies volunteering their memories
Amazing life of coincidences
Writing influences.
The Heat is on.

Accommodation, Airbnb, in the village
Comfortable, breakfast provided;
Food, cereal, bread, fruit, melon,
Pineapple, delicious, sitting in the garden
Dehydration, drinking water, constantly.
Sunburn, slather sun cream Factor 30, minimum.

Writing with Chrissie, work, writing
Too soon, Writing Retreat over.
Kindness, helpful, writing achieved
Encouraged, research, research.

My time is up, time for home
My taxi, station bound, awaits.
The Heat has gone.
Time to write, write, my book.

Kate A. Harris

Dive into a poem

The Sage Said...

'Plant your bum on that chair
Wipe your brow, push back your hair
It's been a tough ride to get to here
Times when you've wished you could disappear
But it's OK, it will all come right
And you will be stronger, because of this fight.'

So spake the sage to me
Passing over a cup of tea
But the pack of biscuits was not proffered
But put away, safely coffered
I managed to dodge the attempted hug
The sage took the rebuff with a sage-like shrug
So we sat in quiet contemplation
There being no need for more conversation

'Don't keep your feelings held down
They'll only wind up, and twist you round
Let out the frustrations
Embrace the sensations
Spread your wings, and fly
In the freedom of a new sky,'

So spake the sage once more
As they moved out through the door
And so their image thus degraded
Even as my sight of them faded

What!!

EE Blythe

Dive into a poem

Dive into a poem

Greek cats

Greek cats are worldly wise.
They know the streets
the corners under steps
where best to bear their kits.
They know the legs of tables
where to snap up scraps.
They stare and do not budge
willing the dropping of a crumb
a fish tail or a bit of fat.

Greek cats own the place
always strutting on the prowl
tails held insolently in the air
unloved unlovable.
Greek cats have no masters.
Cretan cats are undecipherable.
their long nose, their aloof eyes,
you would swear they once ruled
the palaces of pharaohs.

Wendy Goulstone

Dive into a poem

You Belong To Me

See the Pyramids along the Nile
Watch the sunset on a tropic isle
And take on board this sound advice
Never put your head in the mouth of a crocodile

'cause that's the sort of thing he'd do
Just for the adrenaline rush
He's Rubin the miniature dachshund
He's black and tan and daft as a brush

We got him when he was really tiny
He hails from Oxford's mean streets
He was attending Jesus College
Where he was studying squirrels and doggy treats

Sometimes he makes himself invisible
Or just hides away under the stair
And if he's really quiet
It's hard to tell whether he's even there

We buy him toys with a squeaker
But sometimes even these he'll refuse
And he'll sneak off where he can't be seen
Oops there goes another pair of designer shoes

His mom and I take him to the park
It's really good to be together
But sometimes he goes nuts and slips his collar
And he'll run off to bark at a pigeon feather

We make up cute names for him, especially when he's good
Like Ruby-doo, Ruu Ruu, cuz he's just the best
But when he craps on the landing
We call him a little fecker and confirm him a damn pest.

He's eight years old now which makes him fifty one
You'd think he'd be grown up, and know what to do
But he's still so dizzy and unfathomable
I swear he's got a mental age of two

Dive into a poem

He'll go in the garden and won't come when he's called
Round and round, his tail he chases
The more we shout, he pretends to be deaf
But he can hear a sweet wrapper at fifty paces

Rubin, you're the best of times but sometimes the worst
If I'm seeking happiness you're the key
You drive me nuts half the time
But Ruby-doo you belong to me

I'm just like a father to you
And your Mom's just like your mother
You belong to us
We belong to each other.

Martin Curley

Dive into a poem

King Jack

An old man sits there on the garden path
where once a strong young boy guarded the space
and treated all intruders to his wrath,
kept them at bay, made sure they knew their place.
Now, hunched over, squinting through hooded eyes,
it may seem to you that he's asleep.
Yet unwitting intruders are surprised
when they arrogantly step upon his land.
He no longer has to run and hunt to prove
he is still head of the local feline race.
With bristling fur he shifts as if to move,
to pounce. Determination set upon his face.
A fast retreat, no other cat dare linger.
Then he settles down. The undisputed king.

Rosemary Marks

Dive into a poem

The Park Bench

I'm sitting on a bench
Watching the world go by
Listening to the birdsong
Swatting the odd fly
Thinking of my life so far
Wondering just why

I hear a church bell tolling
Striking out the hours
I see young lovers strolling
With a small bouquet of flowers
The warm Sun on my face
And zero chance of showers

I hear the gentle breeze
Rustling in the trees
The smell of fresh cut grass
That tries to make me sneeze
Sitting on a bench
Watching the world go by

Patrick Garrett

Bird

Bright bird,
what sayest thou to the rising sun
that creeps o'er the valleys green
reveals the shimmering of water
on fields once ripe for planting,
and ocean waves that lap enticingly
fresh as a new tidal sea?

Or when you join the chorus,
birdsong that chimes o'er roofs and steeples
to rouse the sleeping townsfolk,
do you squabble, squawk and fuss
those elegant invaders,
the oystercatchers, the waders
who nonchalantly paddle
through fields once sown with crops,
once lush for grazing?

Sweet honest bird, storms stole your trees,
your resting perch, your comfort shield,
come close and tell me what you see,
how Nature will on me lay blame
when skies grow dark, when light is dimmed
and woe thy nest of eggs is broken and cast asunder.
Can you and I together fly
in swoops of joy, in flocks set free
to find the Summer, where She hides
in her lilac flowered veil,
her cherry blossom dress?

Theresa Le Flem

Dive into a poem

Easebourne

They never said there'd be a wood,
So when a verdant lush enfolded our holiday cottage,
it was a calming surprise.
Walls of birdsong wakened us early—
an unconducted symphony of praise,
then, stepping between the trees at dusk,
as silence fell on the hundred acres,
a deer stepped forth and froze,
unhurried by our trespass,
as if to say: Stranger,
if you tread gently,
You are welcome to share our home.

John Howes

Dive into a poem

Ghost Dog

My old dog got a notion to sail the ocean
I can't stay here he said I'd be better off dead
So he put to sea in an old copper pail
Cop a load of my pail he said

He shook his head and wagged his tail
As he set sail for the Spanish Main
He was a short-tempered miniature Dachshund
And Rubin Blades was his name

He came across some pirates on Friday afternoon
He could see them clearly through the fog and the smoke
But he gave them the slip as he went past their ship
After he bought an invisible cloak from a disappearing bloke

He put ashore on the Isle of Jenny
Where he came across a cat beaming with smiles
'I know you,' purred the saucy feline,
'Weren't you found guilty at the sheep dog trials?

Well them legal beagles came over all lovey dovey
They gave me treats and lots of pampering
But I was dogged by a useless lawyer
And I suspect there was jury tampering

I used to belong to Erwin Schrodinger that's his box over there
He said he was going to lock me in it and I said don't you dare
But he grabbed my neck and thrust me in
If looks could kill I'd have given him a stare.

But I stole his box and made my escape
I am talented, cute and super slick
I've been practising my craft for years
Would you like me to show you a magick trick?

Well you can give it a shot but you won't fool me
I may have a long nose and appear very small
But I am a lion among dogs
And I've been everywhere and seen it all

Dive into a poem

What you're about to see I learned from a theoretical physicist
'You've not seen nothing like this,' the cat began to crow
'You shove me in the box and then lock the door
Then open it again after five minutes or so'

'Theoretical physicist,' huffed Rubin as he stood there waiting
But his curiosity persisted
And when he opened the box the cat was gone
It was as if she had never existed

Martin Curley

Dive into a poem

Another Storm

It is late spring with a warm sun
Having dried the earth in the silent wood.
The bluebells are having fun
Nodding in a calm mood.

With a purple haze of late flowers
Swishing lightly in the breeze,
Broken by heavy downpours, showers
Sweet perfume around the trees.

Amongst the foliage a hedgehog is awake
To discover it's too warm, too soon.
They scrummage through twigs that break.
Difficult food choices by the light of the moon.

That parched earth is no longer dry
When another shower drowns the ground
I think it's the time to wonder why
The baby birds are nowhere to be found.

Did they escape the branches that fell?
When another storm attacked the town?
Quick! Hurry home from the town's wet spell
Before the next heavy rain pours down.

This year the unusual weather is too hot
There's been another violent storm,
Global warming, changing seasons are our lot
As these violent storms seem more the norm.

Kate A. Harris

Dive into a poem

A Trio of Triolets

Snowdrops
Some things there are that bring delight –
Snowdrops that thrust up through the snow,
Stars twinkling on a frosty night.
Some things there are that bring delight:
Icicles shine in bright moonlight
But bulbs bring hope that Spring will show.
Some things there are that bring delight:
Snowdrops that thrust up through the snow.

Rosebud Rescue
Promised potential should not die forlorn
I cherish, take indoors to thrive alive
A wind-snapped bud half-hidden on the lawn:
Promised potential should not die forlorn.
Expansive fragrant crimson comes at dawn.
Negating luckless chance, I make revive.
Promised potential should not die forlorn.
I cherish, take indoors to thrive alive.

If Only
If only they could speak you would not hear
For they've been talking unheard all the time
And still you do not listen to their fear.
If only they could speak you would not hear.
The sign that all's awry is loud and clear:
The future you are forging's not their prime.
If only they could speak you would not hear
For they've been talking unheard all the time.

Chris Rowe

A Triolet is an eight line poem with a regular rhythm in each line. It has only two rhymes, used in a set formal structure. The first line is the same as the fourth and seventh lines. The second line is the same as the eighth line. The first line rhymes with the third and the fifth lines. The second line rhymes with the sixth line. ABaAabAB

The Magpie

At the bottom of our garden
hides a young magpie,
who doesn't seem to want to fly
He always seems to stay down low
That's why we call him Vertigo
He ignores his Mummy when she calls
Instead he pecks at fatty balls
Hooray our Magpie has taken flight
In a flurry of black and white!
In the morning he is back once more
Eating from the garden floor!

Susan McCranor

Dive into a poem

Whiteleaf Barrow – Ridgeway Path

Lying in spring-sun
walk-weary eyes closed
sleep would come easy
too easy.
Many more ridge-miles
tick-tick in our minds.

Between squint-lids
ox-eye daisies
veil the sky.
We lie
wondering who
slept death-sleep here

beneath earth-mound
on this high hill
what ceremonies
grief-laid
him under coverlets
of such pure flowers.

Wendy Goulstone

Dive into a poem

Norfolk Stars

There are no street lights
In my Norfolk village
I walk its late night paths
In blinding blackness

Above me are the stars
Ecstatic in their number
Euphoric in their lustre
Lighting up the coal dark sky with overpowering grandeur

Theirs is an awesome splendour
A wondrous beauty
An enchanting mystery
An enthralling glory

Awe, wonder, enchantment
Splendour, beauty, mystery
A glory which reaches out to enthral the night time walker
Herein is the story of Norfolk stars

Poor is he in spirit who doesn't sense a deeper presence
When confronted with that story
A story which calls us to humility
And conveys to us the beyond
And leaves us silent in the company of something greater

Raymond Brown

Dive into a poem

The Black Crow

There was an old crow who lived in a tree
And he was as black as black as black could be
He wore a top hat that he rested on his knee.
And his hat was blacker than the black bit of a bee.

One day a soldier passed by
When he saw the crow he let out at cry.
You've every right to be scared said the crow,
For I know more about you than you'll ever know.

How can one crow know more about me?
You think I am one but I am more than you see.
The crow looked over his hat and tapped with his beak
Then he glared at the soldier and started to speak.

I am one for sorrow
Two for death
Three for the chill
Of your very last breath.
Four for silver
Five for gold
Six to make sure you never grow old.
Seven for your fears
Eight for your woes
Nine for the coming of a murder of crows
Ten is for all the evil that you have done
And all the folks you have shot with you gun
Eleven is for the reckoning
Twelve is for the sorrow
Thirteen is for the hangman's noose at this hour tomorrow.

Martin Curley

Dive into a poem

Insanity Is

Insanity is: Distorted triangles of thoughts swirling around your head,
like goldfish in a whirlpool of salt water.
Or imagining twenty-four and a half people in a Savoy bathroom,
allowed in by the day porter, not the night porter.

Insanity is: Sleeping in the daytime while driving your car,
because you can't sleep at night, it's too quiet.
Or you convince yourself he loves you, so when you find out he doesn't,
you have a reason to commit suicide or pretend to.

Insanity is: Smoking forty cigarettes a day because a quack of a doctor
tells you that you have a weak chest, and you don't want to believe him.
Or laying in the nude and listening to your flatmate screaming
God-damn fuckers, calming her frustrations and then going to your
room alone and saying God, damn, fuckers.

Insanity is: Eating and eating and getting fat because you have nothing
better to do. And knowing with every bite that if you were doing the
work you wanted to do, there would be no time to eat.

Insanity is: Me and you, and John Lennon and Spike Milligan and Alice
in Wonderland and Marlon Brando and...

Madalyn Morgan

Dive into a poem

A Death in the Family

Small hands have placed
your cooling body by the fire,
on newspaper with the headline: 'Tragedy.'
Little twitching movements in your fur
give false hope, as tiny traitorous fleas
desert your sinking ship in search of fresh blood.
While in the corner of the garden, in the rain,
a man evicts worms from their slumber.
They writhe and wriggle and wait to welcome you.
And the child and the sky weep anew.

Rosemary Marks

Order Of Service

Another Order of Service
To add to the growing stack
White paper evidence that
None of these are coming back

So many people lost
Over so few months all gone
And hidden amongst them
Is proof that you were one

EE Blythe

Dive into a poem

Questions and answers

Why do you want this job?
Soon, we'll have known each other longer than when we didn't.

What are your strengths?
I'd go anywhere, as long as it was with her.

What are your goals?
Probably when she said she loved me.

What is your greatest accomplishment?
Every day. I never stop thinking about her.

What are your salary expectations?
Totally indescribable.

How do you deal with pressure?
There was something about her gentleness,
her kindness, her intelligence.

Describe a situation when you have worked as part of a team.
I hurt when she's away, even though I know she is coming home.

How do you keep yourself organised?
Probably our first kiss. No, definitely.

Are you applying for other jobs?
For many, many years. The clawing loneliness ate away at me
before I met her.

There's a gap in your CV. What did you do then?
Once, when I was out, she planted small flowers in the pot outside my front door. I remember thinking this was the most beautiful thing anyone had ever done for me.

Congratulations. We'd like to offer you the job.
She is my greatest achievement.

John Howes

Dive into a poem

Because Of You

(For the Dakota Sioux woman who saved my life)

I am here because of you.
You did not give birth to me,
I am not biologically yours,
but you saved my life.

*

Obese now, through no fault of her own.
Unable to do the things she enjoys.
When she was young, she exuded life –
and she dived into a river to save mine.

Ill now, through no fault of her own.
Alcohol and preservatives are to blame.
In old age, she held me once more –
and I was able to thank her by name.

Madalyn Morgan

Sleep Well David

Last night near home
I met an old friend
A distant relative
Not seen in a good while
Though once we'd take a beer
Or two on Boxing Day each year.

I was hitch-hiking
To congratulate
A mutual cousin
On publication
Of a cookery/poetry book
But I stopped
To chat with my namesake
Almost perfect of an age with me

We spoke not of the past
Of boyhood birthday parties
Of pantomimes, cinemas
For a shadow lay there
More recent
Of broken marriages
Cerebral embolism
I thought had killed him
Two years back

He looked much shrunken
Shorter now than I
With glasses too
Unbalanced
One lens much thicker
Than the other
And pale
Yet seemed happy
He showed me a new bride
I could see his pride
A little blonde girl
They'd bought a house
For fourteen thousand five
Short of money sure
He asked her if they'd better not

Dive into a poem

Have waited
Did she regret
She squeezed his arm
No

He wasn't over interested
In our new family poet
Understandably
On this his wedding day

Would I see his home?
Why not, my family too.
We went by bus
To our Fenland
A village I didn't know
Nor how to get
To where I had to go.

A creaky gate
We entered
A flat square field
Where nothing grew but weeds
No house
On the four acres
Just a double bed
Spread over a single
Six foot ditch
The bride tucked in
Looked now as if
Yes she might be thinking twice
But her side at least was level
Not over the uncomfortable rut
Where her man would lay

My mum, my gran, like his
Berated him
Fourteen five
Sight unseen
For bare land
Then frantic to help
Began to weed to hoe
He had his life ahead
Had to make something
Of the mess

Dive into a poem

I would have helped
Wanted to
But with my trousers
Creased and pressed
I wasn't dressed
For land work

He smiled at me
Wanly
Nothing more to say
Or see

I woke
My wife's hand moved away
But she was there
How glad I was.
To be alive still
Was something
Something, two years more at least
Than David had
My cousin
I met last night.

David G. Bailey

Rainbows

Rainbows made of butterflies
Illusions so it seems
A universe made of stories
Or reality made of dreams

Deceptions all deceptions
Apparitions in our mind
Mirrors of infinity
Where sanity unwinds

Rainbows made from raindrops
Colours that aren't really there
A destination unachievable
To reach them just despair

A covenant with man
A bow up in the sky
Is it just illusion
Perhaps it's just a lie.

Patrick Garrett

Dive into a poem

Dive into a poem

Dive into a poem

The Big Garden Birdwatch

Pigeons cooing on the path
Blackbird splashing in the bath

Water droplets catch the light
Sparkling just like stars at night

Starlings peck upon the ground
Squabbling over food they've found

Blue tits gathering lots of seed
For the many mouths to feed

Robin sports a bright red vest
Takes a worm home to his nest

Magpies swoop with noisy chatter
Causing all the birds to scatter

Sad to say that was yesterday.
Today's the count. They've stayed away.

Susan McCranor

Dive into a poem

A Flowery Poem

A tongue twister

The Cow Slips when she sees Arti Choke and Honey Suckle,
Making a Butter Cup and Corn Flower sauce,
For Sythia who felt Nettle'd when pushed by Laven Dar
In the Vio Lets area of town.
Tu Lips were pursed as she saw Blue Bell Marri Gold.

The Snap Dragon and Gypse Philia scared the Snow Drop
When they Ground Ivy in Camp I On, cooking
In a Pan Sy wearing their Lady's Smocks.
I said, 'Hi, Drangea is with Jack By The Hedge.

My Bud, Leia, Rose followed by the old Sage
Just in Thyme to see Al Ium, one Aco Nite.
The Dandi Lion dropped his Fox Glove, rescued by Lu Pin.

Blue Bell rang as the Dog Rose with his Old Man's Beard
When Marjor Am and Gar Lic of Vi Ola helped
Pop Py join the ringing of Canterbury Bells.

And three cheers, Juni Per isn't a wallflower
she's dancing with Prim Rose.

Kate A Harris

Dive into a poem

Boy on a Swing

Alone in his garden is a boy on a swing
Flying as high as a bird on the wing
Blissfully one with the sky up above
Intensely alive and completely in love,
Completely in love with being a boy
Singing his thanks for life and its joy

Alone in his garden the years have flown fast
Now an old man he reflects on his past
On the thrill he once knew as a child long ago
When the world seemed so good incredibly so,
Incredibly so he still feels a thrill
For the life and the joy which remain with him still

Alone in his garden he offers his praise
For the great gift of living through all of his days,
Through all of his days both as man and as boy
For loving and laughter and friendship and joy
For being alive his thanks he does sing
As he did long ago as a boy on a swing

Raymond Brown

Dive into a poem

Beach Holiday?

Bodies bronzing in the sun
Bingo-wings and builders-bum
Too-small bikinis
And tiny budgie-smugglers
Oh, the joys of Summer
And the British on their hols

Restful the sound of the tide
Bobbing boats on lapping waves
Too-shrill seabirds call
And gather, mob-style, watching
Keen to share a picnic
And see the chips go flying

EE Blythe

Dive into a poem

Rainfall

One
Big drop
Of rain fell
With full resounding plop:
First of many, falling pell-mell
Without a sign of any stop
A falling onslaught, like this downpour swell
Of overwhelming flooding words – quite impossible to quell –
(Need to pause – take my time - instigate another rhyme.)
That solo drop, with eager others, coalesces in a huddle
And striving there, as more arrive, creates a thriving, shining puddle.
The puddle seeps, slowly creeps, begins to grow and then to flow;
As gravity lures, downhill it pours, by nature's laws released, ever downwards bent,
Splashing, dashing crashing, lashing, mashing, bashing, gashing, slashing, smashing: shower power, ambitious for descent!

Chris Rowe

*Rainfall is a fourteen-line poem with each line increasing by one word until the final and fourteenth line.

Hugging the Trees

We all need a hug
said the notice
Hug a tree.
So we spread our arms
put our ears to the trunk
listened to the sap
pumping in its heart.

Sequoia gigantea
a gathering of kings
solemn for council
on the old hall lawn.

We, their subjects
looked up to them in awe
bowed our heads
and hugged them all
while grey squirrels scratched
in the autumn carpet
on the throne room floor.

Cones curled in our palms
glossy as chocolate
trapezoidal scales coiled
in a Fibonacci spiral.
I planned a forest
imagined giants
searched for seeds
in the secret dark.
Nothing.
The squirrels had other ideas.

Wendy Goulstone

Coombe Abbey November 2021

Dive into a poem

Nothing is impossible

Nothing is impossible
President JFK said
to wish upon the moon
In but one single decade

Temperatures are rising
The forests are on fire
oceans full of rubbish
The future is quite dire

I have a dream
Martin Luthier King Jr said
That vision seemed impossible
before all our doubts had fled

The improbable into reality
United States John Kerry said
Our planet is a miracle
the other option will be dread

Patrick Garrett

Dive into a poem

The 2024 Marathon

Half a million plus, applied to partake this year
That was 578,000 participants, just to make that clear.
Pushing their body to the limits, wheelchairs, disabled
All chased their aims and ambitions in 2024.
World's greatest athletes, world's greatest race.
Who could set the pace?

Take care of Climate Change when arriving
Pay the £31 carbon levy, environment not depriving.
There was free transport, don't forget
When travelling in the capital.
London is always the famous marathon venue
Running, unbelievable achievements on the menu.

Full of emotion I watched before they started
Before they, the few, the elite departed.
The world's best runners to compete.
Absence of last year's winner
A Kenyan tragically died too young.
A talented athlete, his name lives long.

Drama, targets to fulfil, fit, healthy
Courageous, quick, don't need to be wealthy.
Families, friends, cheering, chatting, great support
Worthy charities, Cancer, Samaritans, Dementia,
Age UK, Parkinson's to name a few. Too many.
Memories forever, everyone together to raise money.

They wore fancy dress, as a hippo, a piranha
An inflatable whale, in a shoe, photos on a camera.
Rubik's cube to name but a few.
Fun costumes, to be noticed for their charity
To raise awareness for worthy causes, kind donations of money
Thanks for the generosity, and three cheers, the day was sunny.

Runners from all over the world
Walked, ran, sang, whirled and twirled.
The 26.2 long gruelling miles from Greenwich Park
Since 1981 a million plus completed
Past London's iconic landmarks on the way, The Cutty Sark,
The River Thames, Canary Wharf, views from Regent's Park.

Dive into a poem

Finishing past Buckingham Palace, up the Mall.
Targets, records achieved. Wonderful overall.
The winner, the fastest man, Kenyan, Alexander Munyao,
A worthy winner in the footsteps of the greats
Congratulations to Peres Jepchirchir, the Women's winner
The World record holder also Kenyan, to hold their banner.

A fantastic 50,000 crossed the line at the end
Whether on their own or with a friend.
Despite their aches and pains, blisters galore
Will they return next year, 2025?
I say well done. Amazing stories to behold.
Extraordinary feats of endurance, stories to be told.

Kate A. Harris

Dive into a poem

Phoenix

The story of the Phoenix is a strange one to be told
The picture of this noble bird unusual to behold
He sits upon his ancient nest with nothing to inspire
But then hot sparks fall from the sun and set the bird on fire

Five hundred years of living come to a blazing end
But Phoenix calmly meets his fate as if it were a friend
He shows no pain and shows no fear when faced with death appalling
He knows it is his destiny and fulfilling of his calling

Then all is peace, all is calm, all is turned to ashes
Only darkness marks the spot consumed by fiery flashes
But then a deeper magic works, the darkness turns to dawn
Something stirs, something lives – and Phoenix is reborn

He rises from the ashes, a new bird in his prime
The hold of death is broken, the eternal enters time
The whole creation stands in awe, joy replaces tears
For Phoenix has returned to us to live again his years

Raymond Brown

Autumn

The Autumn leaves are falling
Like the dreams of summers gone
no longer seasons stalling
the leaves now on the lawn

Another year is passing
The Sun is sinking low
Autumn colours contrasting
Await the winter snow

The air is getting crisper
Soon frost upon the ground
Now hear Autumn's whisper
with colours to astound

Wintertime is coming
The falling leaves foretell
darkness and light abutting
In the air a fresher smell

Autumn leaves are falling
Like the dreams of summers gone
Soon Spring will come knocking
Another Summer won't be that long

Patrick Garrett

Leaves

The wind was in a temper
And the leaves were having to pay
It tore them from their branches
On that cold autumnal day
It sent them in a whirlwind
Twirling through the sky
For the first time in their lives
It taught them how to fly.

Ruth Hughes

Dive into a poem

The beautiful Beech

How lovely are the leaves that lie a jewelled green
on the beech trees that form an island in a small wood nearby.
I stare up into the heart of the tree,
and it feeds me with its beauty.
The diffusion of light in streamered beams
illuminates each leaf in a different hue,
depending on how they overlap.
I breathe in the colours and all their beauty.
And it lifts my heart.

Ann Cooper

Dive into a poem

The Tide

A Pantoum

A measurement of time in liquid form
In mid-air pausing like a dancer's leap
The arching smooth wave hesitates to land.
Release then smashes down to shake the shore.

In mid-air pausing like a dancer's leap
There's agitated water scurrying into foam.
Release then smashes down to shake the shore.
Smoothed pebbles grind, sucked back with grating roar.

There's agitated water scurrying into foam,
The wind-flung spindrift spatters through the air.
Smoothed pebbles grind, sucked back with grating roar:
The mingling pantoum lines of tide march on.

The wind-flung spindrift spatters through the air,
The spreading wet fans to a shallow glide
The mingling pantoum lines of tide march on,
The mesmerism of the moving tide.

The spreading wet fans to a shallow glide
To reach our paddling feet before retreat.
The mesmerism of the moving tide,
A measurement of time in liquid form.

Chris Rowe

*A pantoum verse has four lines. The second line of the first verse becomes the first line of the next verse, the last line of the first verse becomes the third line of the next verse, and so on until the poem comes to an end.

Dive into a poem

Dive into a poem

Dive into a poem

Twinkle, Twinkle Little Star

Twinkle, twinkle little star
How I wonder where you are
Hidden from our view by light
Which obliterates the night

Up there in the atmosphere
Stars and planets once so clear
Twinkle and shine out of our sight
Changing our perception of the night

Here on earth, electricity
Which was once ordained to be
A protector in the darkest hours
Now conceals the meteor showers

While up above the world so high
Miles above our earthly sky
Debris from the satellites
Makes our night sky over bright

Twinkle, twinkle little star
How I wonder where you are
Man has polluted earth and space
In his effort to better the human race

Rosemary Marks

Surprising Gain

The river sparkled on its lazy journey
The meadow shimmered in the summer sun
Young mothers laughed in company together
Children played in carefree bliss
All was joy
All was beauty
All was life

Yet I was touched by sadness
For this joy would pass
This beauty would finish
This life would die

So I asked a wise old priest
Why endings?
Why loss?
Why death?

He shared his wise old insights:
Joy in this world echoes greater joy beyond
Beauty in this world reflects deeper beauty to come
Life in this world mirrors life which is more real
Love in this world points to love which lasts forever
So when we die we do not lose
When we die we gain

Raymond Brown

Dive into a poem

Cold Moon

There's a cold Moon arising this December day
Stay warm by your fireside to keep the chill away
The last Moon of the year with its ice cold rays
It will soon be Christmas so the cold moon says

Jack Frost reflects the moonbeams from the grass and trees
The pond's frozen surface shines back the light with ease
My windows don't now freeze with artwork below zero degrees
Reminding me of childhood with draughts and chilly breeze

As fair as a Summer's Moon but as chill as winter ice
Its light welcome to the traveller, to get home will just suffice
Human footprints on its surface, to go back it does entice
The cold moon arises, I'm staying in where it's warm and nice.

Patrick Garrett

Winter Views

Shards of glittering diamonds bright,
frolicking through the velvet night,
forming a carpet of densest white –
this is childhood winter.

Winds of frosted fingers blow,
setting ears and nose aglow.
Making our marks on virgin snow.
Such are childhood winters.

Crispy crunching footfall sounds
of wellyboots on snowfake ground.
Winter images so profound.
In your childhood eyes.

Thermometer tumbling, hitting deck.
Indoor wearing of scarf round neck,
heating bills making us nervous wrecks.
This is old age winter.

Stuttering steps tip tapping on ice,
ending on backside – flick of a dice.
Our old bodies paying a terrible price.
Welcome to old age winters.

Extra duvets, extra vests,
dare not venture from frozen nests.
Give me comfort in eternal rest.
And make of me a snowflake.

Ann Cooper

Dive into a poem

A winter drink

Grey shadows flick across the glass;
A world hidden by possessive night.
Inside, the light burns bright,
Banishing the blackness,
Uniting the inmates against the dark.
"One more for the road."
He smiles.
Who am I to deny this wish?
Anything to keep that darkness back a moment more.

Fiona Fisher

Dive into a poem

Yuletide Dusk

Three golden roses glow beside my gate
December blooms, unseasonal, too late
But as these flowers fade along with light
Usurping colours now invade my sight:
Electronic light surprise
For Christmas visitors' dazed eyes.
A glowing snowman six foot high
Outlined against a twilight sky
And at his foot a toy-filled sleigh
Has stopped to let the reindeer play.
Prancing forms with throbbing noses
Now displace my fated roses.
A conifer with shining lights
Illuminates these flashing sights:
A penguin that is far too fat
Now sports a jaunty violet hat.
What was by day a chunk of wood
At night becomes a Christmas pud
That's nibbled by a winking mouse,
While glowing snow glints down the house.

A bell that twitches to and fro
In rapid rhythm far from slow
Hiccoughs from purple into green
And flicks its lights onto the scene.
A multitude of crazy blaze
Now riots its riches to my gaze:
Vermilion, scarlet, crimson, red,
And hues for which no name is said.
The flashing colours dash and smash
Their electronic festive splash,
Swaggering and scintillating
Coruscating, jubilating
 Silent cacophony
JaZZily, snaZZily daZZling me
     Lights,
While up above a moon serene
Shines down reflecting on this scene
Of rainbowed yuletide eccentricity,
Virus-defying electricity,

Dive into a poem

And when the sun returns I know I'll see
Green spear-tips of the snowdrops by the tree.

Chris Rowe

Dive into a poem

Christmas Past, Present and Future

Christmas Past
I loved Christmas as a child.
Sleigh bells, reindeer, what can I hear?
The anticipation, pretending to be fast asleep
As Father Christmas crept into our bedroom.
He was in full red Santa costume, when we were young.
My sister and I eventually fell asleep.
Early morning excitement, father's new goodie laden boot sock;
A tangerine, walnuts, Brazil nuts, chocolate buttons,
A pencil, rubber, small ruler and tiny note book.
Great times.

Every year a real Christmas tree, the same baubles,
Small pink and blue plastic baskets hung on branches.
Packed full of dolly mixtures, not for long, soon eaten.
Candles precariously poised, dangerously clipped and hanging.
Crackers and flower decorations. Lucky holly behind pictures.
Then, delicious full Christmas roast dinner.
Followed by Christmas pudding hiding lucky silver coins.
Never swallowed by mistake,
Numerous traditions adhered to, back then.
Great times.

Christmas Present
I wake up, there's not the anticipation of childhood.
Preparations of delicious Christmas fare, with family
Wrapped family parcels ready to go.
Shared brunch is the order of the day
Visitors at our son and wife's home
We exchange presents.
The grandchildren, older now and not as thrilled.
Excited, yes as they are always pleased with their gifts
And the useful, handy money to spend as they wish.
Great times.

Dive into a poem

What would my parcels contain?
There are surprises, wonderful.
Traditional Christmas fare cooked by husband
It's relaxing, the remainder of the day, overindulging,
And watching favourite programs on the tele.
A keenly awaited new King's speech this year
The first time, no doubt it will be different.
It's 2023, we mourn our late Queen.
Too soon the day is over.
Great times.

Christmas Future
Our space module has landed in our back garden.
Silently the door opens, we, the family, climb aboard.
The door closes, tightly shut. Immediate take off.
Whoosh! We are transported to Mars this year,
The moon last year. Christmas celebrations await.
There's a new substation, Martel is finished.
I took my longer life pill before transportation.
I feel fine and prepared to travel.
It's 2040, I'm 91, fit and ready to go.
Amazing instant Christmas, many packages to open.
A great Christmas day of celebrations, too soon home time.
I ponder, "Where to next year?"
Great times, I wonder.

Kate A Harris

Dive into a poem

Christmas Story

The joy in children's eyes this Christmas
A sparkle to behold and surely to witness
It's hard to believe there are children alone
No roof for a shelter, no place to call home

Santa is coming, we can hear his sleigh
The jingling bells, Rudolph shows the way
But he can't find a chimney if there is none
No toys for these children, they may never have fun

The twinkling lights, there's joy all around
where ever you look, rejoicing is found
No food on a table, there's no Christmas pud
It makes us all wonder, just as it should

Our children are full tucked up warm in their beds
Parents relaxing in a comfy homesteads
But outside it's cold and so dark you can't see
It's the Christmas story and ever shall be

Patrick Garrett

Dive into a poem

Christmas Snow

The land has raised a finger to its lips;
The hush of snow has fallen to the ground.
I wake in wonder to a white eclipse,
Diffusing light and softening all around.
Familiar sounds are dulled and faraway,
The pistons whisper, car doors muffled close:
My early-working neighbours start their day,
Departing down a track that lustrous glows.
I contemplate the landscape they have left;
Nature's cosmetic, rough-scar-hiding white,
Creates a mask of blemishes bereft
That turns to me a view of pure delight.
Relaxing curves, so mood-enhancing,
Evanescence at its most entrancing.

Chris Rowe

Dive into a poem

Good Old Santa

Look up, look up and view the Christmas sky
Cos Santa and his reindeer are up there riding high.
CV21's the target for his present drop tonight
Though the moon is pale and chilling and the roofs are snowy white.

Hillmorton's waiting children have put their stockings out
That a visitor will fill them there's not a single doubt.
But how's he going to get in from out there in the air?
Just trust the wonders of IT, there's no need to despair.

And when you wake up in the early morning gloom
It's as you knew it all along, he's visited your room
The stockings filled with presents are really no surprise
Just tell your mum and dad – trust Santa and his guys!

Keith Marshall

Dive into a poem

And so we got together

T'was Christmas, I was on my own,
The family all away,
Living now in Canada,
NZ and Galway Bay.

So this was just another day.
I had put up a tree,
Tagged with bits of tinsel and
A gift from me to me.

An early rise, an early walk,
A chat online to friends
I'd hadn't seen in oh-so long.
Next year we'd make amends.

Lunch was planned and in the stove,
A pair of turkey thighs,
But when I went to take them out
I found to my surprise ...

I hadn't turned the damn thing on,
Already half-past two,
And so I ducked to KFC
For something else to chew.

At least I had a fine red wine,
Mince pies and chardonnay,
I downed it all and in my chair,
I drifted far away.

Then came the strangest visitor,
Forming in the air,
Materialised, he kissed my cheek,
While pulling up a chair.

I knew the face, I knew the voice,
It was my younger self,
"Go find your life," he ordered,
"And come down off the shelf."

Dive into a poem

"Shake off the myth of loneliness,"
He whispered in my ear,
"And get some friends around you,
At a party for New Year."

I woke and scribbled down a list
Of everyone I knew,
Me and him and she and her,
And you, and you and you.

And so we got together,
And I got back my groove,
The world is there to welcome us,
If we make the first move.

Geoff Hill

Christmas Story

Susie snuggles up in bed and strains her little ears
Santa Claus will be here soon. It's her favourite time of year
She's written him a letter nearly as long as her arm
Mummy always says wanting nice things does no harm
She's asked for a new dolls house, a pram and dolly too
She's fed up with her old toys, wants to start again brand new
She's determined not to go to sleep. To stay awake till morn
When she'll open all her presents. Then when the papers ripped and torn
She'll beg to play, plead to stay. Then grudgingly trot out
To church. Because Daddy says that's what Christmas is all about.

On the other side of town little Freddie cowers
It's cold, he's hungry and his dads been raging on for hours
He wrote to Santa. Just a note. He doesn't want a lot
Just a peaceful Christmas day and maybe a meal that's hot
He wants his mum to spend a day on which she doesn't cry
He sighs and shivers. Raises his eyes up towards the sky
Please Santa if you're really there. I don't want to make a fuss
If you can please grant my wish and try to surprise us
He falls into a dreamless sleep. He doesn't hear the door
Doesn't hear his mum happily greet a surprise visitor.

Next morning Susie's sulking as she didn't get her wish
But Freddie and his mum are full of peace and joy and bliss.

Rosemary Marks

Dive into a poem

New Year Resolutions

I sit snugly in Valhalla on a buttered Stone of Scone
With two phoenix on my shoulders that are posing for my phone.
On a Pegasean Shergar I've flown through the Northern Lights
And I'm staring down at England's unimaginable sights.
There a herd of crimson unicorns stand ready by my sleigh
And the North Sea's frozen over so they trot across and play
While I swallow dive with mermaids from the rainbows over Wales
While the Midnight Sun sparks colours from the scales upon their tails.
Time's rigidity I'll backwards turn without a doubt or fear
And begin again with relish my mismanaged yesteryear.

Though undisciplined indulgences will stand out bright and clear,
Unbreaking all solutions to those broken resolutions,
This second magic chance I'll seize to set out to do things right
And then pigs' wings sound flapping by in the silence of the night.

Chris Rowe

Dive into a poem

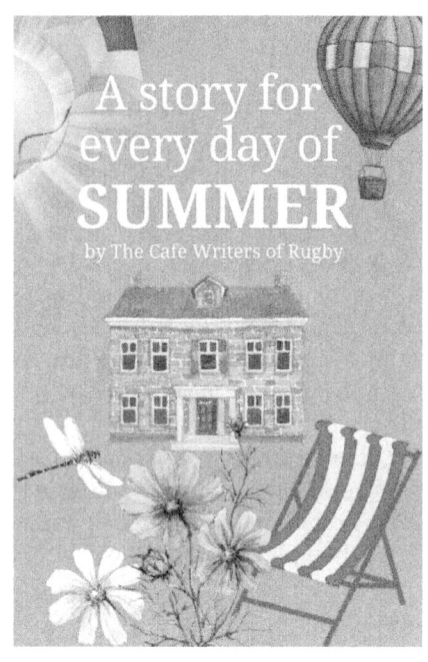

Collect all four of our seasonal anthologies.
Visit us at www.rugbycafewriters.com

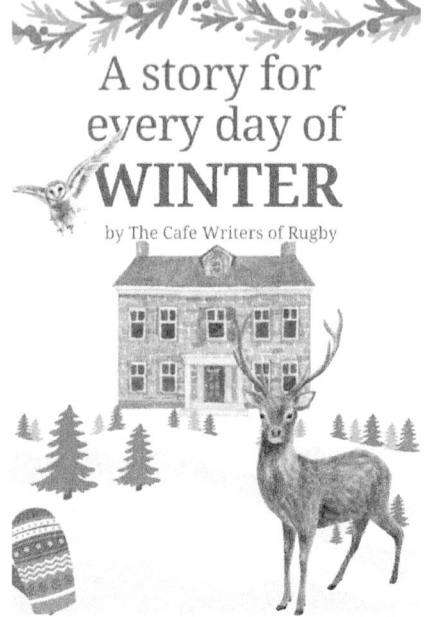

Dive into a poem

Also from The Cafe Writers of Rugby

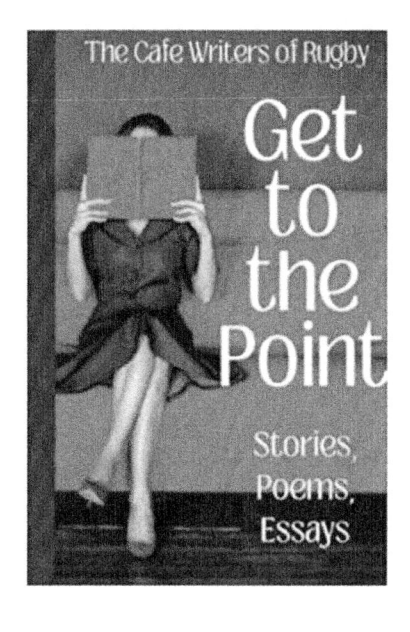

Our first anthology of short stories, poems and essays
211 pages

A thought-provoking collection of poems
251 pages

WHAT OUR READERS HAD TO SAY

'Books to dip into and read an item in just a few minutes, or sit down with for a longer session.'

'It's hard to pick a favourite because they are so different. I'm looking forward to reading more from this group.'

'An easy read. Great as a gift.'

www.rugbycafewriters.com

Dive into a poem

Dive into a poem

Meet the poets

David G Bailey from East Anglia has also lived in Europe, the Caribbean, North and South America, with a base in Rugby for over forty years. While accepting that nothing can beat a good poem, he reckons the odds of writing good prose are more in his favour. He has published two contemporary novels, *Them Feltwell Boys* and *Them Roper Girls*, an adventure fantasy aimed at and beyond young adults (*Seventeen*) and most recently a first volume of non-fiction in *The Sunny Side of the House: When Life Gives You Strawberries - Memories of a Fenland Boy*. To read more of and about David's work, including a quarterly newsletter and new content daily comprising extracts from diaries and other writings, visit his website www.davidgbailey.com.

EE Blythe is compelled to write. And that's all that needs to be said.

Raymond Brown is a retired Anglican priest. He spent forty years working in parishes, mainly in London and Essex . He moved to Rugby in 2019 from his previous home in York. In his school days, Raymond fell in love with the English language and expresses that love today through writing poetry.

Ann Cooper was born in Sunderland and lived in various parts of the North East until she and her husband emigrated (as £10 poms) to Wollongong Australia. One child and two-and-a-half years later, they returned to "the old country". The next move came when the family (by this time four) moved to the Midlands where they have lived for 44 years. In that time, Ann has worked as a marriage guidance counsellor, run bereavement groups for children, been an Education Social Worker and home/school support worker. She is a member of Rugby Theatre, appearing a few months ago as the wicked stepmother in *Cinderella*. She writes poetry when moved and has appeared on *Britain's Got Talent* twice with her performance poetry.

Martin Curley has recently retired from a lengthy career as a long-distance lorry driver. This career allowed him to read many books and listen to numerous radio plays. It also allowed him plenty of time to literally talk to himself, often out loud. This talking out loud usually took the form of two-way conversations of which Martin, obviously, had to adopt both parts. He believes that talking to yourself is the first sign of creativity. These conversations then formed the basis for many of his short stories. He lives in Rugby with his wife and three dachshunds. He stopped watching television about forty-five years ago, citing that ten

Dive into a poem

minutes spent watching TV is ten minutes spent not listening to music.

Fiona Fisher was born at St Mary's Hospital near Rugby and spent most of her formative years in the lovely old library in the town. From here she moved away to study at Royal Holloway University, where she learned the technicalities of language and honed her love for all things linguistic. After almost twenty years as a teacher of English and languages, she is now a Project Manager and looking to finally find the shape for the story she has been germinating for a few years. Her dream would be to win the lottery and open a bookshop so she can spend her days reading and drinking tea.

Patrick Garrett was born in a farm cottage in Perthshire, Scotland before the NHS came to be and spent the first nine years of his life on farms in Perthshire, Peeblesshire, Wigtownshire and Lanarkshire before moving to England, then two more farms in Princethorpe and Dunchurch. His father then moved to Rugby. As Patrick is blessed with mild dyslexia, his academic career was not stellar but once he learned to read, the world became his oyster. His careers ranged from apprentice, shop assistant, removals, HGV one driver and positions in the warehouse industry. He learned to fly gliders then qualified as a CAA Microlight aircraft pilot having his flying stories published in a flying magazine. After he retired, he decided to take up local history research and write about Rugby's history. He then found Rugby Cafe Writers and had his stories and poems published in the Cafe Writers' books.

Philip Gregge was an optician in Rugby for over forty years. After qualifying as an optometrist, he studied theology. As part of the leadership team of a local charismatic church, he enjoys teaching theology and has written a theology training manual for study groups. He answers theological questions in 'Let's Ask Phil', letsaskphil.org Philip started writing Historical Fiction after waking from an anaesthetic with a plot of an Anglo-Saxon murder mystery in his head. This whetted the fascination he already had for the early Dark Ages, and his research led him to write and publish Denua, Warrior Queen 'based on real history, but with some of history's intriguing blanks filled in'. He is now working on a trilogy with his original murder mystery as the first part. In his spare time he plays the banjo in an Irish Music band and repairs musical instruments.

Wendy Goulstone won the Stafford Children's Library playwriting competition when ten years old and was joint winner of Stafford Library's Staffordshire Countryside poetry competition in 2023. A poem was highly commended in the Campaign for the Preservation of

Rural England competition. Her poems have been published in Orbis, The Cannon's Mouth and Hedgehog Press, and long-listed in the *Words out Loud* competition about the Covid outbreak, with a poem in the ensuing anthology, *Beyond the Storm*. Another poem was selected in an international competition and published in *Inspired by My Museum*, with a reception at India House in London. Her poems have been short-listed several times by Poetry on Loan. She is a member of Open University Poets and Rugby Theatre Playwriting Group, where one of her plays, set on a train, was performed on stage in 2024. Her furniture lies under a layer of dust and her culinary skills are basic.

Kate A Harris and her three siblings lived on their farm near Market Harborough. She left home at 16 to pursue her career with children. After training in the Morley Manor, Dr. Barnardo's Home, in Derbyshire from 1966 to 1968, she qualified as a Nursery Nurse. Kate met and married her Royal Naval husband in Southsea when working in a children's home. As a naval wife, she was in Malta for two years with her two sons when they were shutting the naval base. They have two sons and two grandchildren. She worked on the local newspaper and discovered a love of writing at 50! Now she is writing her story mainly featuring Barnardo's. It's a major challenge with intense and fascinating research. She's had an incredible response from diverse and fascinating resources. Kate is interested in hearing from people who worked in Barnardo's, mainly in the 1960s.

Brian Haynes is a member of Rugby Cafe Writers.

Jenny Hicks is Jim's mother. She's an old lady. She normally enjoys doing puzzles and knitting.

Geoff Hill is a Zimbabwean writer and journalist living in Johannesburg. He is chief Africa Correspondent for *The Washington Times* (DC) and maintains a second home in Rugby. In 2000, Geoff became the first non-American to receive a John Steinbeck award for his writing. He has authored two books on Zimbabwe and writes for *The Spectator*.

John Howes was born and raised in Rugby. He was a journalist on local newspapers for 25 years before retraining as a teacher. He has self-published three books including *Driven*, a collection of short stories and poems. He plays the piano and has written music for schools and choirs. John is working on a memoir and more poetry. He runs a book group and a lively theology group. He presents a Youtube Channel dedicated to the music of Elton John.

Dive into a poem

Ruth Hughes was born in Sutton Coldfield but has lived in Rugby for 50 years. She says, "I think I have a book in me but so far I just enjoy writing poems and recollections of my life." Ruth belongs to Rugby Operatic Society.

Chloe Huntington started writing at the age of five or six and since then she hasn't stopped. She has written short stories for school projects and essays for homework, but she has never published any of her works. She hopes that she can one day publish one (or more) of her stories and introduce the world to her world of fantasy, fiction and romance. Chloe lives with her Mum and her five chickens and wants to hopefully write a story from the point of view of a dog that she loves. What will Chloe write next?

Alicja Kulczak is a young aspiring author from Poland, currently living in Rugby. She writes stories about all things dark, real, and alternative; hoping to capture an audience who live for the supernatural and young-adult fantasies. Some of her shorter works try to capture the nature of humanity, and tell deep, meaningful stories through descriptive settings and interesting circumstances. Despite her love for Geography, hoping to study this subject at university, she also has a deep passion for Creative Writing—writing since she was 14. Currently, there's a short-story anthology, and a novel brewing in the background, that she's hoping to serve out in the near future.

Theresa Le Flem, a novelist, artist and poet, always wanted to be a writer. With four novels now published, and also an anthology of her poetry and drawings, her dream was first fulfilled when her first novel was accepted and published by Robert Hale Ltd. She never looked back. Born in London into an artistic family, daughter of the late artist Cyril Hamersma, she has three children and five grandchildren all who live abroad in America and New Zealand. Her creative life began by writing poetry, painting and later in running her own studio pottery in Cornwall. But she has had a succession of jobs too – from factory-work, antiques, retail sales, veterinary receptionist and sewing machinist to hairdressing. Over five years ago, Theresa formed a group of local writers, Rugby Café Writers, who meet fortnightly to talk about their work over a coffee. Writing remains her true passion. Married to a Guernsey man, Theresa shares a love of the sea with her husband and they have bought an almost derelict cottage in Guernsey. Gradually they are working to bring it back to life. Situated only a short walk to the sea, it might one day become the perfect writer's retreat where a new novel might emerge out of the dust and cobwebs. Theresa is a member of the

Dive into a poem

Romantic Novelists' Association, the Society of Authors and The Poetry Society.

Caroline Lucy. After being awarded the children's book *Cat's Magic* by Margaret Greaves at primary school for good behaviour, Caroline's passion for reading was ignited. Failing miserably throughout school and her final English report upon leaving education reading "all too often fails to develop her ideas beyond the obvious", she went into warehouse work. Following this she became a midwife, unhappily worked her way around different areas of the NHS and private health care and had two beautiful daughters and a granddaughter. Her passion for reading and writing never went away and, as a mature student, she went on to gain a First Class honours degree in English and Creative Writing. Her next step is to embark on an MA in Creative Writing. Caroline openly admits poetry 'isn't her thing' and, for someone who can't follow a film, enjoys screenwriting most of all.

A.A. Malik is an established writer published in a range of media. Initially a reluctant poet, her poetry can be found in anthologies and journals and explore the themes of spirituality and motherhood, as well as how ancestry, ethnicity and childhood experiences influence identity, with a focus on multi-sense belonging. When not writing, she can usually be found drinking (or spilling) tea, trying to decipher the hieroglyphs or sweeping legs in a dojo. More at www.aamalikauthor.com

Rosemary Marks has lived in Rugby all her life and has three children and four grandchildren. She has always been an avid reader and was lucky enough to work at Rugby Library for 23 years before moving on to work as a receptionist at St Cross Hospital. Now retired, she enjoys travelling with her husband, writing, painting, researching family history and spending time with family and friends.

Keith Marshall was educated at Cambridge and the Polytechnic of Central London. He worked in production management and human resources in the chemical industry before becoming a consultant management trainer in computers, working in Europe and Africa. He worked in race relations before setting up his own redundancy counselling business, finally specialising in secondary and higher education. As a volunteer, he has been an assessor of hospital care and has facilitated a mental health support group. Within a limited budget, he is a collector of porcelain and watercolours.

Susan McCranor has lived in Rugby for forty-five years. She is married with four children and one grown up Grandson. She enjoyed writing stories to amuse her children when they were small and the children she taught. During lockdown, she wrote some short stories which were read by family and friends. Susan often composes rhymes to celebrate special occasions. Since retiring, she enjoys holidays and days out with her husband and has started a Book Club with friends and neighbours.

Madalyn Morgan was brought up in Lutterworth, where she has returned after living in London for thirty-six years. She had a hairdressing salon in Rugby before going to Drama College. Madalyn was an actress for thirty years, performing on television, in the West End and in Repertory Theatre. She has been a radio journalist and a classic rock DJ on radio. She has written articles for music magazines, women's magazines and newspapers. She now writes poems, short stories and novels. She has written ten novels – a wartime saga and a post war series. She is currently writing her memoir and a novel for Christmas 2024. Her collection of short stories, poems and non-fiction, called *Scenes of My Life, in Poetry and Prose*, is available on Amazon – Kindle and paperback – from August 2024.

Fran Neatherway grew up in a small village in the middle of Sussex. She studied History at the University of York and put her degree to good use by working in IT. Reading is an obsession – she reads six or seven books a week. Her favourites are crime, fantasy and science fiction. Fran has been writing for thirty-odd years, short stories at first. She has attended several writing classes and has a certificate in Creative Writing from Warwick University. She has completed three children's novels, as yet unpublished, and is working on the first draft of an adult novel. Fran has red hair and lives in Rugby with her husband and no cats.

Simon Parker grew up and lived on The Wirral until 1985. He arrived in Rugby in 2003 via Coventry, Bristol and Seattle. He's an aerospace engineer by training, with a love of the open road whether by bicycle, motorcycle or car. His travels galvanise his writing and he writes fiction for pleasure. He lives with his wife, two teenage children and a small collection of interesting vehicles: 'on the button' and ready for their next adventure.

Steve Redshaw was born and raised in Sussex. Over the past forty years he has taught in primary schools in the South of England and East Anglia. Now retired, he is living aboard his narrowboat, Miss Amelia, on the Oxford Canal near Rugby. Passionate about music, he sings and plays guitar in pubs, folk clubs and sessions around the area. He also is a dance caller for Barn Dances and Ceilidhs. His creative output is perhaps best described as emergent and sporadic, but when inspiration strikes, he

Dive into a poem

finds himself writing songs, poems and short stories.

Chris Rowe. Just before covid, Chris tried to write poetry: lockdown gave the time to attempt different poetic forms, some of which appeared in Press Pause. From childhood, Chris has been interested in reading prose: such as Richmal Crompton (Just William), Alison Utley (Sam Pig), Henry Fielding, Mark Twain, Jane Austen, and Terry Pratchett. Shakespeare has always been a favourite and long ago the ambition was achieved of seeing a performance of every play: Antony and Cleopatra being the hardest to track down (all those scene changes deter production.). Favourite performers of the Bard are Oddsocks.

Jeremy Sadler-Scott was born in Norfolk, England however grew up in Belfast, Northern Ireland. After spending fourteen years with the Corps of Royal Engineers, he settled in Germany before returning to the UK in 2007 and currently lives in Rugby, Warwickshire. Jeremy has been in the Self-Improvement and Spiritual Development space for more than thirty years as a coach and has also written an untold number of poems and lyrics under commission and, as a freelance journalist, has written numerous articles for online magazines with a Self Help and Law of Attraction theme. He wrote and independently published his first book in 2018, and his second book is also close to completion.

Dean Speed was born in Telford. Seeking adventure and a break from his humdrum life, he pursued a military career in his early twenties. As he travelled the world, his interest in the arts deepened. Although he had always been a keen artist, dyslexia had held him back in his youth. By his mid-thirties, he decided to expand his creative pursuits to include writing, aiming to broaden his mind and enjoy crafting magical worlds. Now, he spends every possible moment reading, listening, and writing stories and poems. He is currently working on a fantasy novel for his children, hoping to inspire them to write. Dean lives in Rugby with his partner and three children, who already have extensive book collections.

Chris Stanley is a member of Rugby Cafe Writers.

Christopher Trezise was born and raised in Rugby and pursued a professional acting career on theatre stages culminating in work for Disneyland Paris. Christopher has held many jobs from kitchen assistant through to risk management consultant but he has always had a passion for writing. He runs several table-top roleplaying groups which he writes scenarios for and has self-published a fantasy book based upon one of those games.

Dive into a poem

'Red Wellies' - "emotional decompression through the power of words".

Neleh Yartel is a member of Rugby Cafe Writers.

Printed in Great Britain
by Amazon